Counseling Christian Parents

Counseling Christian Parents

by

WILLIAM S. DEAL, M.A., Th.D.

ZONDERVAN PUBLISHING HOUSE
GRAND RAPIDS, MICHIGAN

COUNSELING CHRISTIAN PARENTS

© 1970 by Zondervan Publishing House
Grand Rapids, Michigan

Library of Congress Catalog Card Number 77-120035

Second printing — 1971

Printed in the United States of America

CONTENTS

FOREWORD

Much of the material in this book is in answer to the many questions which have come to me as a Marriage, Family and Youth Counselor over the years. So often people have asked, "Do you have a book with this material in it?" Requests for the material in the chapters on Child Care, Sane Sex Sense, and Troublesome Teens, have headed the list; however, the material in all the chapters has been called forth through counseling sessions and used in the class room and public lectures to young people and their parents.

Written in laymen's language, *Counseling Christian Parents* is not a "cure-all" for the thorny problems of child-rearing by any means; however, the author believes that if parents will take its message seriously and put the rules into practice, they will do a much better job of rearing their children.

If you find this book helpful in dealing with the many problems of child-rearing, why not pass it along, or better still, recommend it to others who may need help?

May God bless the readers, as He has the writer in the preparation of this work.

WILLIAM S. DEAL

Counseling Christian Parents

Chapter 1

Launching a Life

Some wag has said, "Ninety percent of all accidents are caused by humans, and ninety percent of all humans are caused by *accidents!*"

A child needs to be born out of a loving act on the part of the parents who want him and welcome him into the world with tender love and care. Many a child is unwanted from the moment of conception. Sometimes parents make the mistake of telling a child that he was unwanted in the first place, thus dealing one of the most devastating blows a child can receive.

Few other acts of life are more serious than *launching a life* on its eternal journey. From a child's conception to his marriage, his parents have grave responsibilities toward him. Life is no Roman holiday — it is a deadly serious business, and parents need to face this fact as they think of the future welfare of their children.

Someone is responsible for the life of every criminal as well as that of every honorable citizen. Sadly, most criminals are the product of poor parentage and the lack of proper early training. If more children had proper launching and training in life, it is likely that most criminals would never develop. There are, of course, exceptions to that rule, but Proverbs states, "Train up a child in the way he should go and when he is old, he will not depart from it" (Prov. 22:6).

Parents should dedicate both themselves and their children to God early in their lives. Soon after marriage they should begin a program of wide reading on child care and training. Just as it is necessary for professional people to train themselves for their work, so parents also should be trained for this most important life's work — rearing children. To be successful parents, they will need to spend much of their early time after marriage in this research and reading program. This book presents the fundamentals of good child-rearing and proper training. Other books which could provide great profit for parents are listed in the bibliography and suggested reading list, and are hereby recommended to parents as good reading.

If I were the devil I would want nothing better to help my cause than to keep parents in ignorance as to how to train and rear their children. I would be assured by this act that I had gotten my most successful work accomplished. Nothing is a better ally of Satan than such ignorance on the part of parents. I would know that if I kept them in this dense ignorance for the first ten years of the child's life, I could win the child and direct his ways; I would be assured of his soul. I would reap a final harvest of most of the souls of men.

Henry Brandt, the famed child psychologist, has given some good advice to young parents who wish to begin properly as parents:

> In order to be the kind of parents you want to be, you must first be the kind of person you ought to be. To do so you must (1) be willing to understand, appreciate, and use your strong points; (2) with true humility be willing to identify your weaknesses and seek to strengthen them; and, (3) aspire to be the kind of partner that will contribute your share to a mutually satisfactory marriage. It is such experience that will allow you to enter the gates of parenthood, and go on to build your wholesome personality into the lives of your children as you lead them to the Source of power that has been your strength, even God Himself. [1]

In order to be a better parent one really needs to know of the saving reality of Christ in his life and heart, and become well adjusted as a Christian. One can offer to society in his children only what he has given to society in his own life. Upon the foundation of Christ a lovely and enduring home can be built, but unless parents are Christians, they build on shifting sand (Matt. 7:24 - 29). Proper child-rearing and training requires the best possible home foundations, and there can be nothing better than Christian experience.

It is the husband's responsibility to love, cherish, protect, care for, provide for, and give his wife all the happiness he can. It is the wife's responsibility to love, reverence, cherish, admonish, help and in every way care for her husband to make the happiest possible home for them both. They both contribute to make the home a happy and congenial place into which children are welcomed and cared for with loving tender care. (See I Cor. 7:1 - 5; Eph. 5: 22 - 33; I Pet. 3:1 - 7; Titus 2:4; Col. 3:19.)

Neither parent has the right to "shove the other one around."

[1] Henry Brandt, *Keys to Better Living for Parents*, p. 14.

The husband is never to be "Big Boss," ordering his wife around as a slave; nor is she to rebel against him, giving him the "cold treatment." He is to love her as Christ loved the Church, and she must reverence and help him, even as the Church should be in subservience to Christ (Eph. 5:22 - 33). Children reared in a home of this kind seldom go totally wrong and wreck their lives.

"A harmonious marriage is one of unity and agreement. Husband and wife, dedicated to the task of building a harmonious marriage, must have a clear definition of the meaning of these words." [2]

These "keys" are the ability to agree and disagree without fighting over things, to be different from each other without antagonism toward each other; to be in continual change and yet recognize the firmness of each's commitment to the other as spouse, and to plan for unity and work for peace and harmony in the family.

> Seldom, if ever, do the circumstances of living together transform two people of a marriage into an ever-loving, ever-agreeable, happy pair. . . . A happy marriage involves a much greater challenge than simply finding a partner with whom you live happily ever after because of some strange chemistry that draws and holds you together forever. Soon after the wedding day you realize that marriage is a test of your character. [3]

The unruffled love sometimes found in courtship is soon challenged in a realistic marriage. The story is told about the young fellow who courted two girls — one exceptionally beautiful, the other greatly talented as a singer. Being a minister, he felt that he should choose the girl with the exceptional talent, though she was homely. The morning after they were married he awoke and looked over at her, asleep, with her mouth half open. His heart sank. "Mary," he cried, shaking her hard to awaken her. "Mary, Mary, *wake up and sing!*"

Jean and Frank were a most amiable courting couple. He was always thoughtful of her, alert and businesslike. She was gay and full of life and cooperative. They could not imagine there would ever be a day when each one would get on the other's nerves. After being married a few days, they began to discover some essentials which they did not realize came with the package they called happy marriage. Jean lay awake for an hour or two each night, trying to go to sleep, while Frank snored away like a sawmill. She would shake him into wakefulness. He would try to be patient at first, cuddle her up to him and love her, but was soon snoring away

[2] *Ibid.*, p. 113.
[3] Henry Brandt and H. E. Dowdy, *Building a Christian Home*, pp. 7, 8.

again. Finally, he lost his patience and scolded her soundly one night for awaking him for such a little matter. "Go to sleep, now, and stop your nonsense!" he said, dozing back into slumber while she lay and cried. When they walked anywhere he would finally be going about a good step ahead of her. "Frank, please, can't you wait for me?" she cried one day.

"Quit your poking and come on — there's no time to waste," he bellowed and walked on. Jean immediately saw they needed what their parents had told them they would need after marriage. They had called it "making adjustments to each other." When she mentioned the subject to Frank he said, "Yes, I know; I'm sorry for my thoughtlessness. Forgive me. We'll simply have to do something about it. As Christians, we can certainly work it out." And they did. They became in time a happily married couple. Jean has learned to live with his snoring, and Frank has managed to slow down a bit when they walk together. Marriage adjustments are usually about a fifty-fifty proposition if there is to be complete happiness.

Parents will do well to read widely on prenatal influences which may bear upon the unborn child's life. Possibly far more than the average person is aware, the child's whole future may be structured by these influences upon the fetus (unborn child), before the parents are aware that anything at all is happening. The expectant mother cannot be too careful of her life and conduct during this period, yet she should never be unduly cramped as to work, social opportunities or other normal activities. She should guard against deep resentments, brooding hatreds, emotional disturbances which run deep and are of a spiritual or moral nature, or other psychological experiences which may be disturbing.

Psychologists are by no means sure just how far the child's entire life may be affected by prenatal influences. It is certain from many experiments with fetuses that there are certain areas in which the outside influences can have definite effects upon the child, but to what extent or how far is not yet known. Effective techniques have been developed for studying prenatal behavior at all stages in the unborn child. From these investigations much has been learned, but far more is to be discovered as the processes of investigation proceed and improve.

It is now known, for instance, that the fetus develops what is termed "adaptive behavior" at about eight weeks from conception. The child begins to become responsive to outside stimuli by this time. It is thought that "behavioral development" begins at around this time.

While the nervous system of the prenatal infant is not directly connected with his mother's nervous system, and thus he is spared many otherwise dreadful shocks, nevertheless the fetus is subject to certain outside stimuli and often responds to them. Fed by the umbilical cord, the fetus operates his own blood system, purifying it by circulation through the placenta of his mother, where oxygen and nutrients are also picked up constantly by the fetus.

It is now known that as early as eight weeks after conception the fetus may respond to *sounds* outside his mother's body. By using sounds near the mother's body but not touching it and then checking the heart beat of the fetus, researchers have determined that the fetus is affected by *sounds*. They also know that it is definitely affected by pressures upon the mother's body.

These discoveries may be important in the matter of prenatal influences. For instance, if the parents of a prenatal child quarrel, and harsh, loud angry words pass between them, it is entirely possible that the fetus, even as early as two to three months along, may be affected by this quarreling! Most certainly, it may be much more seriously affected by such behavior when it is six months or farther along in prenatal development. And while the fetus is not attached to the mother's nervous system in any sense, yet there may be certain effects produced upon the child emotionally when the mother becomes disturbed emotionally herself. For example, if there arises a quarrel between the parents, and the mother is greatly agitated and excited, or is hit by the father, there may be effects upon the unborn child which will influence him much later in life. (See *Psychology and Life* by Floyd Ruch for more details.) [4]

From heredity we receive our physical features, motor skills, intelligence, sensory acuity, and other fundamental abilities and capacities. But there are other things, such as character or personality traits, which are most largely the result of our environment, especially in the early, formative years. As early as 1890 Professor James of Harvard University spoke of the environmental influences of the child, as follows; "The baby, assailed by eyes, ears, nose, skin and entrails at once feels it all as one great, blooming, buzzing confusion." [5] From this "confusion" he gains all his early environmental concepts. We may close these remarks by saying that the external influences and emotional impacts upon the unborn fetus are so great and the future of the child may so likely be influenced by these, that

[4] Floyd L. Ruch, *Psychology and Life,* p. 32 ff.
[5] *Ibid.,* p. 39.

for the child's sake no parent can afford to risk quarreling, unkindly treatment, or any other types of unbecoming behavior. The impact may be far more disastrous than we now realize, beyond what the simplest discoveries have revealed to date. Parents of unborn children should therefore live as normally as they can in love and happiness with each other.

Certain "old wives' fables" once existed to the effect that intercourse during pregnancy was dangerous to the unborn child. However, all scientific evidence points to the fact that normal intercourse during the first several months of pregnancy is utterly harmless to the child. The fetus is sealed in its own sac, and except for its contact with the mother through the placenta, by which it draws its food, oxygen and blood purification, it is in no way physically affected by any other contacts with her body. In fact, normal intercourse, by which the mother is made happy and contented, may be a *helpful factor* in developing an emotionally healthy child. Parents should be careful not to damage the child just before birth by any act which may affect it. During the last few weeks before the child's birth, intercourse may well be refrained from, or carried out in such a manner that it will not result in harm to the fetus. The family doctor may be consulted for further information and advice concerning these matters.

It is well known that the head is first formed in the fetus. The heart is the first organ to become active, starting to beat possibly as early as the eighth week of its life. [6] The torso then forms, and the hands and feet are last to become activated. But these are activated long before birth, and many movements occur from the eighth week onward.

There is one observation which most parents have failed to think about — the *shock* of being born! For nine months the baby is housed in absolute security, with no temperature changes, no wrestling to make someone know that he was hungry, no need for certain types of bodily eliminations, no need for food or for any other form of security. Then, suddenly, he is expelled into a world where all these things are demanded of him. He is spanked, likely, into his first crying as soon as he is in the world. He is rudely *shocked* by the sense of pain and excitement the first moment he is in the world. He soon senses cold and change of temperature from his accustomed closeness. He is in a large, spacious world, with no sense of the cozy closeness he previously had. He must yell for his food and often is hungry or thirsty the first few hours

[6] *Ibid.,* pp. 36, 37.

or days. No wonder the shock is so great for him. It is quite possible that many people, if not all of us, never entirely recover, even in a lifetime, from the fears, insecurities, and emotional problems that simply being born brought to us! If one could have his full senses and understand what was happening to him, in being squeezed, pulled head-first, and paddled into this world, the shock of it might actually be too acute for him to endure! It is entirely possible that this shock expends its effects over one's whole lifetime.

Some workers in the field of *dianetics* and mental health believe that if every emotional upset and mental disturbance and other such experience of the mother could be correctly traced throughout the prenatal period, mental illness could be much more easily cured, even prevented in the children, or even adults, of such mothers. Enough investigation has been made to convince these workers that bound up in the prenatal influences of the parents upon the child, there is a profound bearing on mother-child relationships throughout the total life of the child. While parents should in no case become frightened about this aspect of child-bearing and rearing, they should nonetheless give this factor thoughtful consideration. And they should so conduct themselves as not to bring upon the child any undue heritages from his prenatal life. [7]

At least one source, Dr. Biddle, suggested that the probable reason why some babies cry and are frustrated when taken up from the crib by the mothers is that the mothers have a "fundamental though probably unconscious dislike of children and a dislike for the feminine role, based on long hidden painful experiences in . . . early life." [8] This inner feeling on the part of the mother can be sensed by the child.

Prenatal preparation for the child's coming is also important to the welfare of the new baby and its future life. Sentman has asserted:

> Sometimes during the months of waiting before the birth of a child, parents unknowingly prepare the wrong kind of welcome. They may have their hearts set on a blue-eyed girl or a brown-eyed boy and are disappointed when their long-anticipated daughter is a son, or junior is a little girl. . . . All parents want to live again in the lives of their children. There is the little daughter who must become the singer mother longed to be, or the son who is to become a football hero. [9]

[7] See L. R. Hubbard, *Dianetics, the Modern Science of Mental Health.*
[8] Doreen Shaw and Bertha Johnson, *Your Children,* p. 13.
[9] E. A. Sentman, *Child Training, A Guide to Successful Parenthood,* p. 7.

Further, there must also be the preparation of the parents for the fact of necessary changes in the home, especially with the coming of a first child or a child following the others after they are well grown up. This preparation is much more important than most young parents-to-be are aware of before the baby arrives. A young expectant mother came to me for counsel. Her first child was about two years of age, and she expected the second in a few months. She reported that her husband was already getting his "feet set" and "bracing" for the coming of this new baby. He had been rather jealous of the first baby because he had been robbed of the attention the wife had formerly given him, and he did not welcome a repeat performance. He needed to mature a bit, certainly; but also the wife needed to realize that not all her affection and attention were to be bestowed upon the children. Many young mother-wives make the mistake of concentrating solely upon the children. Some husbands make the necesary adjustments, but others are not quite able to accept the change without considerable disappointment and sometimes quarreling. Sentman makes an excellent point in relation to this matter:

> During the months before the baby comes, it is wise to prepare for the adjustment required by having the baby in the home. If the baby is a first child, mother and father will have to share each other with the baby. . . . If the young mother becomes completely absorbed in her new baby, the father may feel pushed out. It is wise to think together before the baby comes, to share in plans both before and after his birth, so that the new father feels included from the beginning. [10]

If the child is adopted, the same rule as above should be applied to his relationship.

Some psychiatrists and doctors believe that the attitudes and emotional behavior of the expectant mother may have much to do with conditioning the child's personality, and may show up in later life. For instance, if the mother has tended to be morbid and look at the dark side of all things, the child she carries may also become a melancholia subject or may develop a manic-depressive state later in life. At least there are possibilities that such results may occur.

When the baby is a second or later child, the other children should be prepared to receive him with a good welcome, not shut him off. Sometimes even the tiny baby may become aware of hos-

[10] *Ibid.,* pp. 7, 8.

tilities toward him. He may thus be poorly conditioned for later life, as he may also learn to *fight back.*

Norman Williams has given some wholesome advice for the mother who tends to over-love her child and forget her husband's needs for love and attention:

> The new baby brings new joy, but sometimes because of a foolish, selfish mother, his coming introduces tension and unhappiness in the home. It is a great temptation for this new life to become the all-absorbing object of the mother's attention, until the husband feels himself all but forgotten. Such fastening of a mother's love on a new born baby may dim her love for her husband. Let the new mother be careful to bring her child into her love for her husband. It was this deep, *shared love* between husband and wife that gave the little one life and brought him into the world. . . . If the wife breaks this precious fellowship and the child is set up as the complete object of her love and attention . . . an unnatural situation develops which is full of serious consequences for husband, wife and child. . . . In the case of the mother's doting upon the child, the father is denied the wife's love, and the child is denied some of the father's love; it makes an emotional widow out of the mother for she has cut herself free from her husband's love and affection. The child grows into adulthood an emotional misfit, with a deep sense of insecurity. [11]

The father must remember that the birth of a child is an energy-draining experience for a mother. Under these circumstances she may not always be as energetic as before the coming of the child. He must be patient with her, sharing the household duties and helping her to regain her natural strength. He should also learn to help care for the new baby and thus impart fatherly love to it. The father must also remember that the bearing of a new baby often dims the mother's interest in marital relations for some time. She needs to restore both psychological and physical aspects of her being, and the husband must be tender and patient, showing true love and devotion to his wife, and awaiting the time when she will be more interested in normal sexual relations. If he shows restraint, self-control and tender love for her during this time, he will receive far more affection and cooperation from her when she can enjoy marital relations again. A husband needs to consider this fact thoughtfully. Insisting on one's "rights" to this experience when the wife feels least capable may dampen her love for a long time, or maybe for good. Here is one situation in which self-control pays big dividends.

The wife who truly loves her husband will, of course, not refuse the sexual relationship indefinitely, using child-bearing as an excuse

[11] Norman V. Williams, *The Christian Home,* p. 14.

for avoiding the relationship. She must realize that the coming of the new baby in no way changes her husband's need for her as a marital companion. She will therefore try to return to a normal life as soon as she is physically and emotionally able to successfully do so.

For a splendid discussion of all the problems of prenatal effects on the baby and how the mother should conduct herself during pregnancy, see pages 146 - 162 of *Good Health, Personal and Community*, by B. F. Miller and J. J. Burt, medical doctors.

Chapter 2

Child Care

Much has been written about child care, most of it good. The famous Spock baby books are good, and many others give helpful suggestions. To point up more especially the Christian aspect of child care is the purpose of this chapter, as well as to point out certain moral values which must not be overlooked.

A good beginning is to note John Wesley's bit of quaint advice about child-training. He is reported to have advised, "Never give a child anything for which it cries." This rule may at first sound cold and heartless, but it is actually realistic. It means simply that the child must be taught to secure his wishes by requesting them, but never by *crying* for them. One would except of course tiny babies who cry for food. Even when a tiny baby cries for attention, teach it as early as possible to get this by other methods. Even the small child can be taught that he never receives anything by crying. Children who learn that by crying — and later by temper tantrums — they can get what they want from parents, are well on the way to ruin. If they are allowed to persist, they will soon learn that by wheedling, whining, crying and temper tantrums, they can get their way. As they become older they become bullies, pushing, shoving and demanding their way. As husbands and wives, they will know no better way to get what they want than by such tactics, changed a bit. They will whine, storm, pout and demand their own way just as in childhood.

When parents allow a child to rule them by such methods, they are only preparing the child for a life of sorrow, and sometimes for the life of a criminal. Many a criminal was "conditioned" in his childhood for the criminal role he later played in life.

Few parents are aware of the great importance of child care for the future welfare of a child. A lady recently told me of a grandson of hers who was largely reared by a baby-sitter. Without the proper care and loving attention of the mother, the child developed without any sense of moral and ethical values. By the time he was school age, little could be done for him. Today he is little less than an outlaw, with no concept of life's higher values; his philosophy of life is to "live off others." America is now reaping the frightful harvest of the baby-sitter reared children of World War II, when thousands of mothers abandoned their children to baby-sitters and went to work. Many of these children are now hardened criminals, and thousands more, while making fairly acceptable citizens, have little sense of proper moral, ethical and social values, to say nothing of religious values. A national survey of the children who were largely reared by baby-sitters would produce some astounding facts.

One of the most important things a child needs is the constant loving care of the mother. Children badly need security, which is conditioned largely upon proper love and care in the earliest part of their lives. A family had better live on the ragged edge of poverty while the children are small and have the constant loving care of a mother, than to have all that heart can wish for and be starved for affection and care from the parents. Many working mothers do not realize what they are doing to their children. As a counselor I often find young people insecure, full of fears and frustrations and without a proper perspective of what life is all about. In almost every case these young people tell me of a lack of parental love, understanding and care; and in most cases, too, they say their parents have told them little or nothing about the great and important facts of life. Parents who are too busy during the infancy and early days of their children's lives to give them love and care, and to explain to them what life is all about, are far too busy to be parents. Such young people should decide first, either to put off having children till they can afford them, or to live on less and give the children the attention and care a mother in the home should give them.

Such mundane things as baby feeding and diapering are important in forming the young life. Dr. Jean C. Phillips has some good advice on baby feeding:

> Childhood feeding problems can be frequently traced to a too-rigid schedule in infancy. The appetite of a baby varies from time to time just as does that of anyone else. If a solicitous mother should insist that all of each feeding be taken as has been prescribed, an antagonism to food may develop, and may be the beginning of an emotional disturbance in regard to food. [1]

Babies are "people" — treat them like this and you will make them much happier. By this we mean what Shaw and Johnson point out about feeding them, for instance; "None of us like to eat the same food constantly, yet many babies are fed the same foods in the same manner, over and over. A change of food will stimulate gastric juices and help in digestion." [2]

On the matter of loving the baby the same authors say that, the first thing you can do for your baby is to hold him closely and warmly. Born into a world of strife and chaos, he will need the reassuring love and security you can give him. Do not be afraid of "spoiling" him. You do not spoil children by loving them. From your warmth and nearness your child will receive security which will, if you respond to his further needs, be the first step in producing a well-adjusted child. [3]

Prayer is vitally important to even the very young child, according to these authors. They recommend "praying aloud each day when your baby is in your arms or in his crib; noting that while he does not understand the words, the Holy Spirit will nevertheless indict them to him and he will receive certain spiritual benefits. This practice has been tested to have real influence over him in the days to come." [4]

Children should early be introduced to God as their Father and Jesus as the loving Friend of all children. "Ye are of your father, the devil," was not said by Jesus to loving children, but to hardened older people who had rejected Him. But Jesus did remark that in heaven the children's angels do "behold the face of their Father." All children have a keen sense of God when they are properly introduced to Him. This early training does not mean that they will not later need to be "born of the spirit" to become Christians, as

[1] Jean C. Phillips, *Better Homes and Gardens Baby Book*, p. 6. This book should be read by all mothers.
[2] Doreen Shaw and Bertha Johnson, *Your Children* p. 23.
[3] *Ibid.*, p. 15.
[4] *Ibid.*

indeed they must be (John 3:3, 5, 7); however, it will better prepare them to accept and believe this fact when they are old enough to know it for themselves.

To illustrate the faith of a child and how he sees God in everything, someone has told the story of the child who was looking out the upstairs window one morning when the sun rose. "Good morning, God!" the child said as matter-of-factly as if Christ Himself had been standing nearby. Children have vivid and often powerful imaginations which are helpful in aiding them in religious worship.

The child should be taught to *obey*. Obedience is one of life's most important lessons. Unless the child learns to obey he is headed for all kinds of problems. Most hardened criminals were children who never sufficiently learned the lessons of obedience, nor why it is necessary. The place to correct "criminals" is not in institutions, but in the crib, the playpen, and in the home environment! Children who learn well their lessons in absolute obedience will not likely have much trouble obeying the rules of good society and the laws of the land.

Shaw and Johnson have put this well:

> One of the first steps in disciplining a child is teaching him what he may and may not do. It is totally unfair to punish a child for wrongdoing when it has not been made clear to him what is expected. God the Father set down the boundaries for our first parents. . . . You cannot imagine a just God punishing man for wrongdoing that has never been clearly explained as wrongdoing. [5]

How important this is in childhood has been pointed up helpfully by two other good writers. Ella Frances Lynch once said, "If you train your children carefully until they are seven years old, they are already three-quarters educated." Clarence Benson adds a note of warning: "Upon this foundation the subsequent physical, intellectual and spiritual structure will be built. Failure in the superstructure will naturally result when the foundation is not properly laid in the early and most impressionable years." [6]

Lewis E. Lawes, long time Warden of Sing Sing Federal Prison, once made the stinging remark: "When we get to the place where we pay more attention to the *high chair*, we will have less need for the *electric chair*." [7]

There can be little question but what we either win or lose the

[5] *Ibid.*, pp. 73, 74.
[6] Clarence H. Benson, *An Introduction to Child Study*, p. 91.
[7] *Ibid.* Italics mine.

child to the cause of good and upright future living by the time he is ten years of age — some say seven — as a general rule. How important these tender years are few parents seem to recognize. These are foundation building years and we cannot afford to treat them lightly.

Not only is obedience necessary, but the art by which it is secured in children is also important, as may be seen in the following illustration: Brandt and Dowdy tell of two mothers trying to teach their children not to spill milk, and illustrate the approaches to teaching obedience: One mother told her child, "If you spill your milk, I'll spank you." The child, or course, spilled the milk and was spanked. The other mother simply said, "Don't spill your milk, dear," and proceeded to show him how not to do so. If he became careless, she tried to help him avoid spilling it. Occasionally, the child defied her and spilled it intentionally, causing the mother to spank him, saying "No, we do not spill our milk." This latter way is far better in teaching the child the lessons of obedience. The "spank" or punishment method should only be used when it is absolutely necessary. The first mother took the *negative,* while the second one took the *positive* approach to gain obedience. [8]

The effectiveness of early child training and its consequences can be seen in Benson's illustration of the Jewish people:

> The Jewish people are one of the greatest mysteries of the world. A nation as old as the Chinese, but without king or country, scattered among the nations, yet not assimilated by them. But for the key of scripture they would remain the great mystery of the ages. . . . Joseph said to his people "Our principal care is to educate our children, and we think it is the most necessary business of our home life." Philo, a pagan before his time, also said of the Jews, "The Jews look upon their laws as a revelation from God and they are taught these holy laws, so to speak, from their swaddling clothes by their parents, masters and teachers." [9]

If American children had this sort of upbringing and careful training our nation might also survive untold centuries, but with the careless way in which many children are being reared, the future of America seems at times dark indeed. How could all the abandon of riots, looting, pilfering and wanton destruction of property by gangs be carried out in America if children had been all properly trained in youth? There is no place for such anarchy in the Christian way of life. This, then, is the fearful result of un-

---

[8] Brandt and Dowdy, *Building a Christian Home,* pp. 103, 104.
[9] Clarence H. Benson, *An Introduction to Child Study,* p. 74.

trained children breaking in maddening fury upon us. If children are not trained properly today, there may be little more than a chaotic civilization tomorrow. It will pay parents big dividends to train their children correctly to respect parenthood, know moral, ethical, social and religious values and to learn proper respect for law, order and the love of land and liberties.

Williams points up four important principles in the child-training program. 1. Start early. 2. Be practical. 3. Be patient ("Fathers, provoke not your children to wrath"). 4. Have faith, doubting nothing. [10] If these principles were adhered to by each parent, the world would never get over the results of just one generation of such child-training and rearing. Someone has well said, "Discipline is a lost word in our generation." Williams adds that "discipline is required in the life of a child if he is to be well established spiritually, moderate emotionally, socially adjusted and happy personally." [11] The word of God has guidance at this point, and as we study His Book we shall be grateful for its wisdom.

The matter of teaching obedience in child-training is so important that much has been written about it. On the point that parents must be clear in their own minds as to why they demand obedience, Sentman says:

> Many parents fail to get obedience from their children because they themselves are muddled as to why they want obedience. Some parents make obedience an end in itself, instead of asking for it only when it is necessary for the well being and safety of the child. Try to teach obedience only in important matters, such as insisting that the child stay within limits. Trying to teach obedience in itself can make a child timid and lacking in initiative or rebellious. [12]

Demand obedience only in matters that are important enough to make some difference in the child's life or safety or health. Avoid demanding obedience for every trivial thing. Otherwise, the child is confused and upset. Sometimes parents demand obedience, then later disregard it. This inconsistency confuses the child. "Why did you ask me not to go out into the yard yesterday, then don't object to my going today, when it's just the same?" Can you answer that, intelligently, parent? If not, then do not make it a demand.

Obedience should be demanded only when lack of obedience involves the rights of others, is not good for the child, is against his safety or health.

[10] Norman V. Williams, *The Christian Home,* p. 102.
[11] *Ibid.*
[12] E. A. Sentman, *Child Training, A Guide to Successful Parenthood,* p. 59.

Do not *yell* at children — speak mildly to them. If you need to raise your voice, do it earnestly, but calmly, and *never in anger*. Anger only begets anger. "A soft answer turneth away wrath: but grievous words stir up anger" (Prov. 15:1).

Do not demand obedience when the child has his own rights and carrying them out is in no way wrong. For instance, give a child freedom in stacking his toys, choosing games to play with, meeting his friends, giving greetings, talking to his friends. Do not demand that he act in certain ways, when it makes no moral difference whether he acts this or that way.

Obedience should never be demanded in situations involving nervous habits such as thumb-sucking, frequent masturbation, nail-biting, hair-twisting, failure to go to sleep, fears of any kind or even the difficulty of sitting still. These cannot be stopped with a command because they have developed as a result of a child's anxiety, concern, or unhappiness. They can be cured only when the cause has been discovered and the child's anxiety has been lessened. [13]

Parents should seek to find the cause of nervous habits and work to cure the cause, not merely scold and beat the child. This action would only drive these habits farther into his consciousness and make them even worse, developing a guilt complex, and possibly paving the way for really serious problems in the teen or later years.

Obedience, parents must learn, teaches the child responsibility and dependability, and should never be taught for the satisfaction of the parent alone. One may so break the will and kill the initiative of a child by the demands of absolute obedience in everything, that he becomes docile and useless. In later life he will demand and need guidance in almost every decision he makes; he will never be secure and able to stand on his own, but will be always ill at ease with others, nervous and fearful, and afraid of life. Many parents have killed all initiative that a child ever had and left him almost a vegetable to be a burden to himself and others through life. Some have laid the foundations for mental ill health in later life by over-demanding obedience. To say to a small child who is nervous, "Sit down and be still," and later, "If you don't sit still, I'll beat the stuffings out of you," is to demand something God Himself would never demand of a child. Make your demands for obedience few and see that they are kept.

Contrary to the ideas of persons, most grandparents can often do a far better job of rearing children than younger parents. They

[13] *Ibid.*, pp. 59, 60.

give the children *love* — which every child needs — and make fewer demands, often with more and better explanations of the demands which *are* made. It is then easier for the child to see and obey. Most children dote on their grandparents and will often love and obey them more than their own parents. Jealous parents contend that it is because the grandparents "spoil them rotten!" In reality, it is only because the grandparents have more sense than the parents about what to do. Observe this simple fact: Often a child comes home from spending a vacation or summer with grandparents a much more calm, reassured, and unruffled child than when he left home. The reason is not far away, and sensible parents would do well to take a few lessons in child rearing from the grandparents.

When children are bossy, bully others and fight a lot, the reason may be excessive energy, which need not give the parents great concern. However, sometimes parents need to see what is "eating on" Junior if he fights a great deal. He may be unhappy, need more loving attention from his father or mother, or be suffering from a sense of insecurity. If these problems can be corrected, the child may fight less often. If brother-sister fights occur now and then, don't interfere unless one child is really harming another in deep anger. Siblings will usually settle their scores with each other and do a much better job without parental intervention than with it. I grew up in a family of six — three boys and three girls. We fought and scratched each other, but no one was hurt, and we are all very close and loving today. No harm was done.

Tattling is a normal experience of pre-schoolers and should be looked at as such by parents. Don't scold and berate; simply explain that this is not nice behavior, and help the child to see that he would not like this done to him. When someone else tattles on him, then point out, "See, this hurts: don't do this to others."

Bad words are common. Don't wash a child's mouth out with soap, but put pure words in his mouth instead. Explain the use of bad words as something naughty that will make others dislike him. Read to him that Jesus said we must give an account at judgment for all lies and bad words, and that God will require clean language of us. If the child persists, be more stern and possibly deny him a privilege. Use corporal punishment as a last resort only.

Sex play causes deep concern to many parents. If a child is caught looking at another child's sex organs, do not scold him, but explain that he need not do this. Answer his questions about the other child, especially if the other child is of a different sex. Explain that this is the boy-girl difference, that God made people this way, and this is what makes boys and girls *different*. If children's questions are answered as they come up, the matter usually takes care of itself. Try to keep a watch on children without their knowing it. Try to see that sex play is not too frequent. Sometimes it is wise to undress brother-sister teams and place them in the bathtub together where they may play and have fun and become acquainted with each other thoroughly. Then explain to each one, separately, the functions of the penis and the vulva, using always correct names for these organs. Do not give them *more* information than they ask for; give it only as they ask. Thus their curiosity can be satisfied and a parent will have few other problems.

Forbidding children to play with each other, scolding and making them think they are *sinful* or *nasty* are the worst things you can do to them. They immediately develop a sense of guilt and shame, along with a deeper desire to investigate even further and more often. Then, too, shaming may instill a deep sense of guilt about sex that will persist in girls far into womanhood.

Frequently, little girls from five to seven years of age are observed playing with the vulva and report getting pleasure from this experience. Those who counsel with older girls and ladies have found that numbers of them received deep sexual pleasure from this experience as early as five or six years of age. This fact is nothing to be alarmed about; furthermore, it is something one cannot do much about without damaging the whole structure of the child's life. It likely indicates that the child has normally been given to a strong sexual desire by nature which sometimes subsides by puberty; however, it sometimes remains for life. In such cases one simply points out to the child that she is not to be continually fondling herself, just as she does not rub her eyes all the time or blow her nose all the time. One should explain that it is much like scratching her back when it itches, but that she does not go around scratching her back all the time. If one gives the impression that this act is sinful and wicked, the child is only driven into secrecy and even deeper into the habit; by simple explanations and recognition that she probably has this problem, by helping her to understand and curb it, she will likely master the situation and no harm will come of it. The act itself is physically harmless, all doctors and social scientists report. Any harm that may come is in the overdoing of it, the development of a psychological compulsion for such an act, or from a religious guilt-complex, if this aspect is overemphasized. This same principle also applies to boys who may later develop similar habits during the teen years. Teach them to keep well bathed and keep the sex organs clean, for cleanliness will help to hold down the amount of irritation which sometimes triggers the problem in the first place.

Psychiatrists and social scientists do not believe that homosexuality is inherited or comes from any deformation or malfunction of nature, but is an acquired habit. There may be certain weaknesses in children which can cause it to develop, but it is not inherited. Shyness in boys, fear of girls, and later, a deep hidden fear that one cannot function as a marriage partner may be causes for homosexuality, but it can be cured if caught early enough. There is no need of the child becoming one of the more than fifteen million homosexuals now in the United States. Girls, too, need to be watched as they develop into sexually capable life from fourteen onward. Ten to twelve years of age is a period suggested for an explanation to children of how homosexuality starts and the dangers arising from it.

Imaginary playmates are an important part of almost every child's life — especially where there may be only one or two children in a home. Our daughter, Evangeline, had an imaginary husband and children in her childhood. Her husband's name was "John Lewis" — in the days when John L. Lewis was popular as a labor leader. This fantasy did her no damage and she finally married a popular young minister, after obtaining her master's degree and teaching awhile. His work has led him through the doctoral program to a successful professorial and ministerial life, so perhaps her idealistic playmate was not too bad for her!

Parents should never discourage children in their fantasies. If children build no air castles, they will likely never build any real castles in life. This fantasy-play is important in a child's life; often marriage and child-bearing plays an important part, especially in the little girl's states of development. It is only the mother instinct asserting itself healthily at an early age. Possibly if this trend is not cramped but rather encouraged, it may forestall the older girl from a premarital pregnancy, for in her childhood days she may work out of her system the innate desire for motherhood in fantasy which may spring full blown upon her in the mid-teens and become a passion almost ungovernable, if it has been cramped in childhood.

Family standards should also be included early in life. When a child misbehaves and says, "Well, Mommy, Jack does this all the time; what's so wrong with it?" it is best to simply reply, "John, our family does not do this; this is not part of our way of life. It is not best for us to do this, understand?" Likely he will say either, "Oh, I see," or "Boy, I don't understand!" Then, instead of thinking him stupid and dumb and willfully disobedient, sit down and explain to him in simple language why you do not do these things. If you gain him, you have won a glorious victory. If he still persists that he wants to do what Jack does and sees no reason for his family's old foolishness, then simply inform him that he may have a few days to think it over for himself, and then he must report back what he has decided. If his decision is good, praise him generously for using his head and thinking. If it is adverse, then simply explain that you are sorry, but that he must obey you till he can see what is best. At this time he cannot see what is best. He will know then that you really have been fair with him, and then will generally accept your decision, if your demands are reasonable. Some children are born with a strong will and must be conquered either by gentle or more severe means, but they must be brought to see the reasons for the demands of obedience, or they will never develop into good, obedient children and later, law abiding citizens. Your child will likely never have any higher standard of moral values than you teach him.

When there are other "difficult" children in the area, it is best not to forbid your children to play with them altogether. Teach them to get it across to the other kids that the price they must pay for playing with them is that they must behave nicely and act as they should. Get them to visit you and have a good talk with them. Try to understand why they are naughty and what is behind their actions. You may be able to understand and help them, whereas by cutting them off from all social fellowship with your children, you may even drive them farther down the road of despair. Never give in when your youngster wants to accompany other youngsters to places where they should not be. Try to help the needy youngsters develop more wholesome attitudes toward the right way of life. Your own children should have been taught obedience so well that you have little trouble with them by the time they are old enough to be going out at night and running around with other teen-age friends.

Good manners are best taught by parental example. Get good books on manners; teach children polite rules of etiquette and conduct as early as possible. Good grammar, for instance, is far more the result of its continual use by the parents than of what the school can teach children. So likewise are good manners. About once a week have a dress-up dinner for the family and put on the best of manners and demonstrate to them *how* they should act.

Then praise them when they act well in public, and don't scold them when they fail, but gently remind them that they did not draw an A for their good manners, and to try for a better grade next time.

The *oldest, middle* and *youngest* children in large families have the hardest roles to play. As the oldest child, I recall vividly the sweltering southern summers when I had to attend to the younger children, diaper and feed them, care for them and be a second mother. Often the middle child has problems because of both older and younger children, and the last one is sometimes spoiled by the others, though he, too, is often left with the extra chores by all the rest, who want to go somewhere or who have extra duties. Parents should try to equalize the loads of responsibility and help to make family life more tolerable for all, as far as possible.

Parents need to help their children become acquainted with the great *fears* of life and understand them. All children must sooner or later face these fears, and they need to be prepared for such experiences. Parents should help the children to understand that there is really *nothing* to fear in life, except bad *people* and bad *things.* They should condition children to understand and accept illness in the family as well as going to the hospital and to the police or other officers of the law. Fear of darkness should be explained as the "fear of the unknown"; children should be taught that darkness is a great blessing, providing for sleep and rest. They should also be taught the good fears of life, such as the fear of not being cautious enough, and therefore, having accidents and being hurt; or the fear of doing wrong things and getting punished for them; and the wholesome fear of God.

Children must early be taught that they are not to be destructive with their own or another's things, that this is wrong and they must not do it. Likely their desire to be destructive is a signal that there is something wrong in their own minds. They are insecure, afraid, or hostile toward someone or something. This hostility needs to be corrected and brought out by the parents. Once brought into the open, often the hostility ceases and the destructiveness in over.

Temper tantrums are matters of serious import in children. Perhaps they are suffering from something deeply upsetting or disturbing or are afraid of something or someone; they may also be trying to get attention in this way. Parents should seek the cause for such actions.

Tantrums are in no sense to be condoned or allowed to develop, for they tend to grow on one and must be stopped. Beating is hardly the necessary way to get children over tantrums, although there are a few times when other measures fail and the strap is the only method left. The child who is whipped must understand fully that he is being whipped for the actions in the tantrum. He should be taught to master his temper. It is a good thing if his ambitions and will power are harnessed and used for good; if allowed to run free, they may wreck a child. Point out to him that many bad men who are now in prison for killing people were once just boys who did not control their tempers. Now, they are ruined for life because they did not control their *tempers.*

Children must be taught that they are not to *talk back to their parents* in a naughty manner. They should be given opportunity, however, to explain to the parents why they disagree with them when they are required to obey. No parent has a right to yell at his child, demanding obedience, when he refuses to explain to the child *why,* when the child is fully old enough to understand. Even a six-year-old can often demand an explanation for his obedience and be justified in doing so! Talking back to parents is a form of child hostility, and parents should so understand it. They should encourage free speech, but not tolerate haughty back-talk. By talking back children vent hostility on the parents. They should find another way to work off such hostility. They should be allowed to speak out as they feel, or to discuss the matter quietly with either parent. If the situation is allowed to go too long, the child has forgotten what he was hostile about. The sadness of the problem is that the hostility attaches itself to the subconscious mind and may remain there for life, if not dislodged. Many a person has been utterly honest when saying he did not know *why* he was hostile toward his parents. He has never quite gotten over the hostility developed in childhood which was never allowed to vent itself. It has been buried in the subconscious mind and later vents itself in various ways.

Chapter 3

Life Is for Love

Children are not only the *products* of parents, but also the *projections* of parents. Love is the fundamental and basic principle upon which a successful home is built. This principle needs to be operative at all times in the home. Love is not always the showing of affection in tender kindness, fondling, or other physical expression of affection. It sometimes comes out in sternness as well, when necessary, and often proves to the child the loving care of the parent just as well as the expressions of affection.

The future happiness of children is quite largely conditioned in the early home life. They will either reap a harvest of blessing from this condition or be warped and twisted into insecure, fearful and unhappy people as they become adults.

Home life is largely what the parents make it. It is the business of parents to *make a home* for the children, not the children's business to create the atmosphere of the home. Parents can make that home a window of heaven or they can make it an adjunct to hell. It is up to them what they want to make of it. If they start by securing the right companion and begin marriage with a family altar and loving considerations for each other always, they can build a home which will stand fortified against all the devil's onslaughts.

Here are a few rules which if adopted early and followed carefully will make for a happy and successful home.

1. *Let love be the governing factor in all things.* Whatever plans are made, see that nothing will counteract love and bring a shadow of disappointment to the home. The parents generally start out as a loving pair and intend to remain that way. But as times goes by various pressures build up and it is often easy to allow irritations, short patience, cutting words, and thoughtless deeds to creep in. Where once love reigned supreme, now there are misunder-

standings, brooding, pouting, and cross words. These problems should never be allowed, for they bring shadows over the home that may linger throughout life. One can sometimes hurt a companion so deeply with bitter, hot, thoughtless words that he or she will never recover. Control yourself!

2. *Welcome each new baby with delight.* The new baby should have been started on his way out of acts of love and tenderness, and he should have the privilege of being born into a home of sunshine and love where he feels wanted and loved. It is perfectly possible that infants may be able to detect if they are unwanted in tones of voice and the way they are treated. Harsh words or being left alone unduly for long periods of time by the mother, may cause the child to imbibe even in infancy the notion that he is unwelcome. One is amazed at what is now being learned about the baby's ability to learn about his earliest environment and its influences on him.

Beyond doubt, many of today's neurotic children and insecure, fearful young people are the results of the lack of loving care in childhood. Love is important to the child.

3. *Make the home the early training center for the child.* The Scripture, "Lo, children are an heritage of the Lord . . . " (Ps. 127:3) means that God has given us our children. We have a tremendous responsibility to give back to Him, properly trained, the life with which He has entrusted us.

Many parents never think of the home as a *training* center. It is merely a shelter for the night, an eating place, and a place to go when there is nowhere else especially to be! This is our modern tragedy. We are now paying a high price for this attitude about our homes, but we have not even begun to reap the harvest that awaits us if we as homemakers do not change our attitudes and policies about home life.

Home is the most ideally fitted place on earth for training of all kinds. The parents stand as go-betweens in a child's relation to God. In fact, to the small child the parents represent the image of God. "My Daddy can do *anything!*" a small tyke boasts, and he feels as deeply as adult Christians feel that God can do all things. The parents are the moral and religious guardians and directors of the young child's life. All the ideas about God, righteousness and morality are instilled into the child from the parents and other adults in the home or the family connection. Often times when parents are non-Christians there may be an aunt or a grandparent or other relatives or friends who may impart Christian ideals to the child. But if there are no other such persons to impart this knowledge and these ideals, the child grows up without them. A child without a sense of moral values can very easily turn into an adult with no sense of true values in life such as justice, fair play, honesty, and moral integrity.

Out of these childhood timbers is made the hard wood of criminals and misfits for life. If parents do not train their children rightly and they fail to get good training from other sources, what other hope is there for them to ever receive it? What non-Christian parents need to realize is the frightening fact that *paganism* is only *one or two generations* removed from the total lack of Christian training! Even Christian parents need to consider whether they are doing a good job of true Christian training.

Children should not only be taken by the parents to Sunday school and church, but they should also be provided with an abundance of good religious and moral character-building books. Children are easily influenced by what they read. Fill their minds only with comics, salacious literature, the regular diet of many TV programs which are totally inadequate as well as emotionally unwholesome, and leave them without the influence of Christian books, art, and music, and what can you expect to produce — pagans!

Parents need to see that children are given the right kind of moral, social and religious training, whatever the cost.

4. *Be stern with children when necessary.* Bradley was a tall boy of fifteen whose parents were Christians. He came to me for counsel, complaining that he did not know whether his father loved him. "Why, Brad, what's the problem?" I asked.

"Well, Dad never corrects me. He says I'm a good boy and don't need any correction. But I know a boy of fifteen must make *some* mistakes and need correcting sometimes," he explained. "If he would just correct me sometimes for things, I would be more sure of myself. The way it is, I suppose that he loves me, but I have no way to really know."

I helped Brad to better understand his father. Together, we worked out a system of things to do and not to do for a boy of his age. He then wanted me to talk with his father and help him to understand that he needed correction to be secure. But the father was hardly the type of man who would have profited by such instruction, though he was a fine man otherwise. This father did not see what his soft and affectionate manner of treating his son was literally doing — or undoing — to the boy. I counseled with Brad over a period of months, giving him the needed attention which he did not get from home. He became a well-adjusted young man and made good in life, for awhile; but later developed mental problems, possibly due to the lack of parental love.

A father complained in a husband-wife counseling session that he had to be away from home most of the time, and that his wife refused to punish the children when they needed it. She said, "I want the children to love me. I don't want them to grow up feeling that I was always the one punishing them."

I explained to her that she was actually *driving them away from her* — not drawing them to her, by her failure here. She was totally unaware that uncorrected children come in later life to all but *despise* the parent who allowed them to grow up in this manner. Perhaps you have read stories like the one of the young man who had gotten into trouble and was in jail. His mother went to see him, weeping and pleading that she had done her best to show love for him. "Mother, there's no need of your crying over me now," he said to her in his distracted manner. "If you had only properly punished me and made me obey you when I was small, I'd not be here today!"

Young people sometimes report that their parents have failed to correct them properly, and that they feel insecure because of this lack. A young woman reported in a counseling session that she had indulged in a certain type of childhood misdemeanor and was never properly punished for it by her mother. "I suffer from a terrible sense of guilt now. I want someone to beat me till I'm black and blue; or, if I could do something so bad that my church would turn me out publicly, so that I would be punished for my wrong-doing, I think I would feel better." Here was a case of paranoia in reverse — where the person is not afraid of persecution, but actually wants it. It is the sense of need for punishment for unrelieved guilt. I was able to help her back to a more normal state of mind and emotions. This case helps to show what actual *damage* parents can do to their children by failing to correct and punish them properly.

The notion that children should never be punished is contrary to both the Bible and sound child psychology as well. "Thou shalt beat him with the rod, and shalt deliver his soul from hell" (Prov. 23:14). "Withhold not correction from the child: for if thou beatest him with the rod, he shall not die" (Prov. 23:13). "Train up a child in the way he should go; and when he is old, he will not depart from it" (Prov. 22:6).

On the other hand, there are some sadistic parents who beat their children unmercifully. Naturally, such actions are detrimental and even dangerous to the child. In every case where children are punished, there should be the proper mixture of affection and sternness so that the child is fully aware that even though he is punished by the parent, the parent also loves him very much.

Children should never be told they are wicked and mean and that the devil will get them. It is sad that for years some parents have told their children all these ugly, bad things about themselves, until they are almost totally wrecked emotionally. One of the worst things a mother can say to a ten-year-old girl, for instance, is, "Mary, you'll never get a good husband. No man would want to marry a girl like you — you're a slow brat, and no good for anything!" Or, a son is often told that he is a no good, will never be worth a "hill of beans," and other such things. These are detrimental suggestions. By the time the children are in their mid-teens they are so insecure, afraid of life, and emotionally disturbed that little can be done for them. They fail their studies at school, are poorly adjusted in society, and many of them suffer for a lifetime because of such suggestions by their parents. From these circumstances, many a young person has turned to crime, immoral conduct, or dope.

The child should be given a better view of his future by being made to feel that he can make good in life, and by expressions of confidence that *he will* do so. When twelve-year-old Joey Barnes got himself into some trouble at school, his father heard about it and they had a little session. Joey admitted his part in the misconduct and agreed to right it the next day.

"Now, Joey, that's fine, but I'm going to have to punish you for this. You knew better. Some day you will possibly be the president of a big corporation, or maybe the United States Senator from our state. I'm going to do my part to see that you make good," the dad said as he laid the lashes on young Joey's back. Joey never forgot those kind words. The whipping burned only a few minutes after it was over, but those golden words of confidence for his future lived on in Joey's heart for years. And sure enough, one day Joey succeeded just as his Dad had predicted — probably, largely because of the way in which he was reared!

The same lesson applies to girls. Girls may have a higher ratio of insecurity and fear than boys do generally. If when mother applies the rod of correction she also adds the prophecy of a bright, successful future for Betty, she will do a thousand times more good with her corrections.

5. *Parents must remember that their children are largely the projection of their own lives.* God said long ago, "The fathers have eaten sour grapes, and the children's teeth are set on edge" (Ezek. 18:2). "Like father, like son."

Just as certain physical likenesses are passed on to children by their parents, so are other characteristics which children receive from parents. If parents are dishonest, insincere, hypocritical, or otherwise unsound, the children will often take on this coloration. Occasionally, where parents have been immoral or hard drinkers, the children will revolt against this type and become instead upright and sober persons. But many of the traits of parental character are projected into the children's lives. It is important, therefore, that parents not merely *tell* their children what to do, but *do* the right things before them. Someone has well said, "Example is ten times stronger than precept." Parents who want to have good children to offer society must themselves be good examples.

Possibly the story of the father and son in the snow has come to your attention. As the father left the house on a snowy morning he heard a wee voice behind him. Turning around, he saw his son. With radiant face the little fellow cried, "Daddy, I'm stepping right in your tracks!" The father thought for a moment of his own life. These words hit home. He realized his son would walk in his tracks in a far more important way than merely in the snow. The father turned to Christ that he might direct that boy in the right way. How many other parents should do likewise! If you are not a Christian parent, please give Christ your most sincere consideration. Or, if you are a professing Christian whose life is not as exemplary as it ought to be before your children, attend to this matter at once. There is far too much at stake to neglect it longer.

Children are products of early environment. Parents need to be aware that many small things they do and say may influence children for a lifetime. To illustrate, an intelligent young lady complained in a counseling session that she was suffering from some type of unnatural fear. "It usually comes about sundown and lasts till well past dark," she explained.

"Is this fear fairly constant?" I asked.

"Well, it tends to come and go, but it's worse in the spring and early summer, for some reason," she explained.

"Did you have any shocking childhood experience, like being left alone by your parents, or being badly scared as a child?" I asked.

She thought a moment, then blurted out, "Yes, but I had never thought of it as having anything to do with this. When I was a wee tyke Mother took me with her and left me securely fastened on the shore of a river; then she went swimming. I remember now that she did not come back till about dark. I was scared so badly that I remember it yet, how I feared she would never return."

"What time of year was this?"

"It was in the late spring or early summer."

"There, then, is the basis of your current fear," I explained. "It was pushed down, hidden in the subconscious mind. It would rise just sufficiently to trouble you with deep personal fears, but not sufficiently for you to associate it with the memory of this experience."

She reported later that all those old evening fears had cleared up entirely. When the emotional surge would arise to be afraid, she recognized instantly what it was, and it soon ceased to exist.

Many adults have similar experiences, only far more serious, which have been carried over from childhood and the earliest environment in the home. Some of these hidden experiences are so deep and severe that persons suffer mental breakdowns. Many others, not quite so deeply affected, suffer severe maladjustments emotionally and otherwise. Parents should be careful never to leave small children unguarded, nor to scare them with scary stories about bears getting them, and other such tricks which unsuspecting parents sometimes do to their children. They may be *conditioning* the child for a life time of suffering unless he is able to overcome these frustrations, either by himself or by professional help later.

6. *Parents should show love for each other before their children.* Many young people reveal in counseling sessions that their parents seldom if ever show any affection to each other before them in the home. Children need to witness the show of affection on the part of their parents and to feel something of the warmth of its fire in their own hearts. Younger children especially feel much more secure when their parents manifest affection to each other in their presence. The absence of these little acts of kindness, affection and fondness leaves the children rather cold themselves. They also often wonder just where the parents stand with each other — do they *really* love each other?

Children are very susceptible to affection. They literally drink it in when it is shown to them; they have a high ratio understanding of love and its place in life, too. They need love and they freely give it to others. Normal children are naturally loving towards others of their age. Often they show considerable affection toward older people, if they can be assured that their affection is both accepted and returned by the older person. A child can also be definitely offended by the rejection of his love by anyone, especially, an older person. A child has a keen sense of need for affection and a deep sense of appreciation for it.

Some parents feel that the show of affection toward each other in the presence of the children may be too suggestive. They fear the children may get wrong ideas about sex life if they are too affectionate — especially in such matters as kissing and embracing. *Nothing could be farther from the truth!* It is almost universally true that children do not associate the sex act with the expressions of affection on the part of their parents. The younger children who most need to see these expressions of affection for the sake of their own security do not know about these things in the first place. Teenagers and older young people have an understanding of sex life and usually think either that their parents are very happily married, or that they are allowing their love to show through. Even if all the children were fully aware of what the whole realm of affection meant to the parents, this is only normal married life at its best. How could the normal happily married life, demonstrated in tender affection, possibly be unhealthy for the children, even if they know the details of this life? Will they not soon all look forward to a happily married life, and would not the parental example be a wholesome pattern for them to observe?

Parents who hold such wrong opinions about their love life before the children should rid themselves of these as soon as possible. *Life is for love,* and the more of it that is expressed properly and in good taste before the children, the more emotionally healthy and happy the children will be.

> Love is not passion, love is not pride,
> Love is a journeying side by side,
> Not of the breezes, nor of the gale,
> Love is the steady set of the sail.
> Deeper than ecstasy, sweeter than light,
> Born in the sunshine, born in the night,
> Flaming in victory, stronger in loss,
> Love is a sacrament made for a cross.
> — M. V. H.

Children also need the sense of spiritual security. They feel this need at times quite strongly, as is illustrated by a story Martin Simon told about Princess Margaret of England in his book for parents: "When Princess Margaret was five years old, the newspapers reported that she came out of church one day bitterly disappointed. The minister's prayer had disturbed her. 'Why did he only pray for you and Daddy and Elizabeth?' she asked her mother. 'I'm just as bad as you are!'" [1]

Some people think children live carefree lives with never a worry about spiritual things, or even about eternity. But they often do,

[1] Martin P. Simon, *Points for Parents*, pp. 127, 128.

even at five years of age and younger. The adult department of home management is often responsible for much ignorance relative to these things, from which many children later suffer.

7. *Avoid quarreling before the children, but discuss things freely.* Younger children do not understand what is happening when parents quarrel — especially when they use sharp words and seem angry with one another. Even a good lively discussion with disagreement and loud talking is often emotionally disturbing to children. Teen-agers are also upset by the quarrels of their parents. There is always an uneasiness produced by the quarrelsome atmosphere, however much parents may say they love each other. Often teen-agers feel that the marriage is not a success, and they either never want to marry or become convinced that this is the *norm* for marriage. Either conclusion is unfortunate.

When matters arise which demand discussion, discuss them freely with each other in a calm manner. If the discussion gets out of hand and is becoming more of an actual quarrel, then *cut it short right there!* Change the subject. Calm the children's fears and help them to accept the fact that discussions are a *necessary part* of family life. Make it a rule, if you must quarrel, to arrange to leave the children and go somewhere alone to fuss it out. This is a poor solution, but it may be better than holding it in for days, or *pouting* it out, and demonstrating before the children this utterly *childish method* of trying to solve a problem!

Two intelligent, adult people should be able to discuss matters sensibly and come to some kind of workable plan or conclusion. Quarreling over matters, hurting each other with caustic words and charges and counter-charges, is utter foolishness. It should be avoided as one avoids other childish things. Children need to hear sensible discussions of matters about home life and even parents' affairs now and then. But don't you think it is a bit on the "stupid" side to be constantly quarreling as first described? Then, make it your rule never to resort to this way of settling problems. Remember, nothing is really *settled* by quarreling. Each such hurt tends to drive a couple farther apart; so, stop it now, or better — never allow it to start, if you are young parents.

8. *Apologize when necessary.* Parents often need to apologize to each other for things they say or do which have hurt the other. If one has hurt the other before the children, then the apology needs to be made before the children. Some men especially feel that they cannot stoop to apologize to their wives — this is beneath their dignity as head of the home. This attitude is wrong and utterly un-Christian. No one is ever *always right!*

Often, parents need to apologize to their children. Certainly a child knows when he has been unduly mistreated by a parent. He also knows when an apology is appropriate. Never think for a second that you will lose the respect of your child by apologizing to him when you know that you are clearly at fault. Parents should not resort to apologizing for every little thing, however; an apology should be made only when the parent is clearly at fault in what he has done, or has made a serious mistake. For instance, a parent may sometimes, through misinformation, punish a child when he is not really guilty of what was reported about him. In this case, the parent owes the child a thorough explanation and an apology. If another member of the family has been to blame, then that one should receive due correction as well.

Another thing which is important in this connection is that the parent making the apology should do so soon after the event which demands it. Otherwise, the child's short memory will not be able to correctly connect the apology with the event which demands the apology, and its purpose is largely lost.

Children, of course, should also be careful to apologize to their parents when they have been in any wrong which may have hurt the parent or embarrassed him or her before others. Children who learn to respect the rights of others and to apologize for any offense they have made will generally become well adjusted and make the best of good Christian citizens.

9. *Respect the child's rights.* Every child has his own rights in the home. If these rights are not respected by the parents, the child cannot be successfully taught to respect the rights of others. His life will become warped and he will grow up with wrong attitudes toward life in general.

Some psychologists assert that parents should *never take away* a child's weekly allowance, if he has an established allowance. If he has any sort of allowance, this is his money or other property. To take it away from him is to teach him that property or money values are not important. If his allowance is withheld constantly, he will finally decide that this must be a rule of life. So, when he steals from someone else, do not be too hard on him — you *conditioned* him, psychologically, for this very thing.

What should parents do if the allowance has become an established thing and yet some change needs to be made about it? For instance, the father is out of work, and the allowance must be stopped; or, the child has disobeyed an important rule of the home, and cutting his allowance is being considered as a means of punishment.

First, if the former situation avails, sit down and explain to the child what the condition is and that all will have to sacrifice together for awhile, till the father secures work again. But explain to him fully, don't just cut him off with no explanation. The child has feelings, too, and he needs to *share* the situations of the home. He will be better off in adult life if he does share.

Second, when you wish to use the allowance cut-off as a means of punishment, do not *cut it out entirely*. Explain to him that because of his disobedience, you are *withholding* his allowance for this week. This punishment will achieve the same good as cutting it out all together, for he will miss it just as much, but still you have not broken faith with him. This is his money, just as your salary is your money, and he often feels keenly about it. The one week's withheld allowance should be added then to the following week's allowance — unless you establish a little scheme of justice, which may be valuable, too, in teaching the child that he must sometimes pay penalties for his disobedience. If the offense has been sufficiently grave, then the parent will talk it over with the child and he will have to pay this week's allowance into a common kitty kept for this purpose as a sort of "fine" for his disobedience. The child needs to be taught the lesson that one must somewhere, sometime, *pay* for his disobedience. This may be a good way to get this lesson across.

When children are given tasks to do, do not take the task away from them and re-assign it to another without a complete understanding with the first child of what is being done, and *why*. It is important to teach children *responsibility*. If parents assign a task and then for no cause apparent to the child, snatch the assignment away and give it to another, the child soon gets the idea that he, too, can make promises and break them at will. Promises come to mean little to him. His parents can make and break them at will, so why cannot he?

Never promise a child anything which you do not carry through. If you find you cannot do what you have promised him, explain to him fully *why* you cannot, and make him understand that you did not mean to break a promise, but that you are unable to carry it out. If you promise corporal or other types of punishment, keep your word — unless, of course, circumstances have changed so that your plans must be changed. Then, explain fully to him so that he understands why you did not do what you promised. Otherwise, he lives in dread that the punishment will still come, even though it is past the time it was promised, or he may come to regard your promises as meaningless.

Sometimes, when the child has mended his ways sufficiently, you may be able to give him a very *light form* of punishment, explaining to him that this is due to his having mended his way. Even God was known for His mercy in the Old Testament times. There are cases where He threatened punishment, then withdrew it, as in the case of Nineveh. (See the Book of Jonah.)

Make it a rule to always keep your word strictly with your children, or always explain to them fully any changes made and *why* the changes are being made. This *why* business is important to children. Often parents simply tell children it is none of their business *why*. This answer is an *insult* to an intelligent child. He may take it and keep his mouth shut — at least to you — but he will never think as much of you as he ought, especially if he is older and knows there is a reason why, and that you are either too secretive or too stubborn to share with him the reason. You are *losing*, never gaining him, by such treatment. He may come to look upon you with pity and disdain, but not with respect and honor as you most certainly want him to do when he is grown.

10. *Love your children physically when they are small.* Children just dearly love to crawl up into parents laps and snuggle down there. It affords a sense of security such as no other thing can quite bring to them. They need the physical closeness which such loving provides. Often a child will come to a parent and want to be loved. Just a small caress and a tender kiss send them on their way, scampering off full of joy and blessed contentment. All of us who had a normally healthy childhood can remember what joy it afforded to be loved physically by our parents. Those days live on in the halls of memory as some of the greatest times in our lives. Just to be near them, feel the warmth of their love and care was heaven to us then, and heavenly memories now. Possibly one reason we have so many "neurotic families," so much youthful crime and sinful indulgence, is that modern parents have no time to love and play with their children. So, the children grow up without love and understanding. They are insecure and badly need attention. Sometimes, failing to get the needed attention, they try to "harden" themselves and "steel themselves" against all affection. Thus they become easy prey for the terrible "gangs" that form in cities, out of which crime and immorality are bred.

In a large summer camp some girls in their late teens came to talk with me, revealing that they were from "broken homes." Their mothers had not taught them anything about sex life and matters of love-making and marriage. But fortunately, these were good girls who wanted to find life's best. They would meet at noon or after school hours to read good wholesome books on sex and marriage and other such matters. At their meetings each would report what she had discovered from reading, and they would then discuss this. Smutty jokes and senseless talk were forbidden. Occasionally, a girl joining their group would start telling a dirty story. The girls would simply freeze her out with disapproving looks or a stern reminder that if she attended these meetings there would be no such talk. She would either conform and become a good member, or leave the group.

It was marvelous how they had conducted their meetings and had learned in a lofty and noble fashion the necessary facts about life, love, sex, marriage, and related matters. These girls had found a way to handle their problems, even if they had missed the much-needed help of their parents. But this, sadly, is an exception to almost the whole general pattern of those who have failed to receive proper love from their parents.

The lack of proper physical loving in childhood can become a crippling experience for a child. It may blossom out into full blown emotional and even mental problems in later adult life. I have spent endless hours counseling with adults whose childhood lives were starved for affection. Some of them present the most pitiful examples of emotional disturbance. One single young woman in her thirties had developed a deep hostility toward all men. Counseling revealed that her father had said of her in early childhood, "I'm turning her over to you, Mother. Since it appears, that you seem to feel, I've failed miserably with the other children, it is doubtful I can do much for her, either." She could never remember after that that he ever touched her or showed any signs of affection, except on one or two occasions when he punished her. She was a religious person, but her concept of God was one of absolute sovereignty — a tyrannical Being who waited ready at the least provocation to *punish* her. She had also become withdrawn from society and had almost lost her interest in herself as a woman. Everything about sex, in every respect, was totally taboo. She was a gifted writer, a capable worker in her field, and a devout church person. Over three years of ardent work in counseling were required to help her become a normal person. She developed serious emotional problems in the reconstruction of her personality — for that is what was literally required. Her faith in God was sorely tried before it was over.

The transformation of this counselee was remarkable, however, her whole concept of God changed completely — to that of a tender, loving Heavenly Father. She became very feminine, even changing her style of dress and entire appearance considerably. Her whole outlook on life changed and she became a vibrant witnessing Christian. Her feelings toward men changed so that she became comfortable with them; in her work she was better adjusted to society as a whole, as well as to those with whom she worked. Her whole personality became so altered that friends who had known her before the transformation instantly recognized that she was a completely *different* person! She became a living witness to the power of God's grace and the effects of Christian counseling to transform a personality so completely as to make her almost literally a new creature. In fact, she often referred to herself as the Old Jane and the New Jane, so complete was this change. But it was not without intense suffering and almost the loss of mental balance. She has witnessed many times that had it not been for the transformation which came, she would have suffered a complete mental collapse, which is doubtless a true evaluation.

There are millions of persons in the world who have suffered similarly, though not as seriously as this young woman, from the lack of early parental loving. It is almost a crime against humanity for parents to have children whom they do not love physically and emotionally. God has evidently intended that this should be the case with human offspring. Animals and fowls drop their offspring, and in a short time they are on their own. But it takes from infancy until about fifteen years of age to bring a child to the place of self-direction. It requires several years more, then, to complete the task of giving him the total equipment and training he needs to give and receive love, to live life at its best. *Life,* then, is *love;* and in no period does the child need this love so seriously, if he is not to become emotionally warped for life, than the period from birth to six or seven years of age. The most healthy and happy children who make the best adjusted adults, generally, are those who have had plenty of physical loving and cuddling in childhood. Even in the teens children need to be reassured of parental love again and again. They may sometimes *act* as if they want to be independent, but underneath there is still the need for affection and appreciation.

As children grow a bit older this affection needs to break out also into *appreciation* and *approbation,* often expressed. If children do not get these at home, they will seek and find them elsewhere. For example, when Charlie came home with his sixth grade report card, Mom looked at it, screwed her face into a frown and said, "Chuck, what are you doing with those two C's in arithmetic and English? Can't you do any better than this? Don't you know if you don't master these subjects, you'll never become well educated? And my goodness, child, what on earth did you do to draw that D in art?" Chuck went to his room after supper a sad boy, more deeply rebellious than ever. Later in the evening he ventured to discuss this with Martha, his older sister. "Mart, Mom and Dad sure scored me for those low grades. But they never even saw the two A's and the B I made. No matter how hard you work, you never get anything but scoldings, so what's the use to try?" Martha tried to explain that this is just Mom and Dad, and to ignore their reaction and go on. It is tragic, but often the oldest child in a family is almost *drained*, emotionally, supplying the younger ones with the affection they should get from their parents.

Parents need to remember that they should never be so tired, so tied up with other things, or so engrossed in matters of life that they do not take proper time for loving their children. Sometimes children for want of love become physically ill. The lack of love and attention of the parents produces so much insecurity, fear and unrest in the child that he becomes physically sick. Doctors often find children run down, weak, nervous and frustrated, possibly for lack of proper loving and showing of affection on the part of the parents.

For a healthy, and well-adjusted future life, parents, give your child lots of physical loving, constant appreciation and approbation. Give him well-deserved praise all along. It will not make him proud and puff him up, but give him a healthy self-esteem and a bright, cheerful outlook on life. It will solve many of your later problems in life with him if you take time out now in his tender childhood years to truly love him and make him assured of it by many physical expressions.

Dads need to take time out to take their sons to places, show interest in them, play with them, have fun with them, and in many other ways let them know of their affection for them; mothers need to do the same things for daughters. You will have them for only a few short years and will probably soon look back with regret that you did not do more of these things with them; so, take off now while you can. It is more important that parents should *make a life* for their children than that they make a *living* for them.

Love needs to be lavished upon each member of the family, as Simon has well pointed out in the following words:

> We husbands should appreciate what our wives do. Our wives should appreciate us more. Parents should learn to appreciate their children. And carefully so as not to be seeming to be selfish, parents can train

their children to appreciate their parents. Certainly that much-for-gotten ideal of "being lavish in our praise" is part of the little verse which makes such a good foundation for happy homes, "Be ye kind to one another." [2]

Where this kind of love and appreciation abounds in the home, the result will be few maladjusted adults. Half the ills of the world could be effectively cured by love, kindness, sympathetic under-standing, a free expression of deep appreciation, and proper correc-tion in the home when needed.

Companionship between marriage partners is of great importance in any happy and stable marriage. Of this aspect of marriage, Blood and Wolfe said of man: "His wife has become a man's best friend. . . . Companionship has risen to become the single most valued aspect of marriage." [3]

Out of a family research project by Blood and Wolfe, in which 731 families were studied, it was found that disagreements between marriage partners were largely confined to the following areas, with the percentages as listed: children were responsible for 16 percent of the disagreements; recreation, 16 percent; personality problems, 14 percent; while money accounted for 24 percent of the squabbles. Sex in this study was listed lower than any of these for some reason. It is often listed as one of the highest percentages of reasons for disagreements. [4]

This study reveals that if parents are willing to go the second mile with each other in a truly Christian manner they can lower the rate of disagreements considerably. This average was from homes at large, Christian and non-Christian, and if these low average figures obtained in this situation, they could be brought far lower for vital Christians. Companionship is so important to a happy marriage that a pair cannot afford to allow it to be degenerated by useless disagreements about trivial things.

The same researchers also found that children have a healthy effect on parents. "Although children may depress the standard of living and the ability of the couple to find companionship outside the home, they increase the emotional bonds of understanding and love between the partners." [5]

[2] *Ibid.*, p. 154.
[3] R. O. Blood and D. M. Wolfe, *Husbands and Wives, the Dynamic of Mar-ried Living*, pp. 149, 150.
[4] *Ibid.*, p. 241.
[5] *Ibid.*, p. 232.

This study revealed, too, that mothers of pre-school children were more nearly satisfied with the love which they received from their husbands than at any other period of their marriage. This may be because the children draw hard upon the mother's attentions and affections. Husbands should realize this need and try to cooperate accordingly.

Sometimes along the pathway of love and marriage a couple get married who do not truly love each other at the start. It is beyond question for that matter that in every successful marriage the companions *learn* to love each other much more as they work out their marriage together.

The far-famed Narramore Christian Counseling Clinic, Rosemead, California, receives thousands of letters from people needing various kinds of help. Below is a letter which illustrates how a couple may really *learn to love each other* long after marriage, if they will only try. While this letter is from a wife, it might well also be from a husband.

Dear Doctor Narramore:

You often speak of persons who marry in haste or without love, and at that time warn the youth against this mistake.

But this does not much help the persons already married without love. I married to get away from home; yet today, twenty-three years later, I have a happy marriage and home. I'd like to share my solution with you.

In the beginning it was pretty bad. My husband's action in every crisis and in everyday living was inconsiderate . . . or at least I thought so until I took stock of myself. How is an unloved person supposed to react anyway? I gave a lot of thought to this word love as used in the Bible. Can God expect us to love one another if it is not in our power to do so, or if He will not enable us?

One day I was saved and I began to know what God could do for me. Was love something that you felt, something that happened to you, or an act of the will? I finally faced the fact that I might not be able to *feel* love, but why could I not *show forth* love? From that minute on I began to behave as if *I did feel* love! What would I do for my husband today, I asked myself, if I really *were* in love with him? Then, I proceeded to do these little kindnesses. I studied his likes and dislikes and bought little treats for his lunch box. I tried to comfort him when he came home from work tired or harassed by a too heavy schedule. I met him at the door with a smile. I respected his discipline of the children and worked with him. I tried to speak softly and diplomatically when we had differences. I listened to him.

Soon I noticed a marked change in him. He was behaving as though he were living with someone who loved him! And I began to notice a change in my feelings. He was not at all like I had concluded. He had real depth! And I was beginning to fall in love with him! Is this why God admonishes us all to show forth love? He had not said to show forth love if you feel love, had He? At the time it seemed to me that Christians do all the giving and none of the getting. But, when God told my heart to show forth love, it was really I who was blessed at the end.

Only last week my teen-age son said, "All of my friends say that I'm lucky."

"Why?" I asked.

"Because you and Dad really like each other," he said. "You'd be surprised at how many of the kids' parents don't get along too hot."

So, my answer to the people who are stuck in a marriage that was hasty or is loveless is to "Show forth love." [6]

Unsigned

The following is such an excellent piece on child-rearing that we feel it should be included here as a few extra guidelines for parents.

How to Make Delinquents

The Houston (Tex.) Police Department has issued the following "Twelve Rules for Raising Delinquent Children":

1. Begin with infancy to give the child everything he wants. In this way he will grow up to believe the world owes him a living.

2. When he picks up bad words, laugh at him. This will make him think he's cute. It will also encourage him to pick up "cuter" phrases that will blow off the top of your head later.

3. Never give him any spiritual training. Wait until he is 21 and then let him "decide for himself."

4. Avoid the use of the word "wrong." It may develop a guilt complex. This will condition him to believe later, when he is arrested for stealing a car, that society is against him and he is being persecuted.

5. Pick up everything he leaves lying around — books, shoes, clothes. Do everything for him so that he will be experienced in throwing all responsibility on others.

6. Let him read any printed matter he can get his hands on. Be careful that the silverware and drinking glasses are sterilized, but let his mind feast on garbage.

[6] Used by permission.

7. Quarrel frequently in the presence of your children. In this way they will not be too shocked when the home is broken up later.

8. Give a child all the spending money he wants. Never let him earn his own. Why should he have things as tough as you had them?

9. Satisfy his every craving for food, drink, and comfort. See that every sensual desire is gratified. Denial may lead to harmful frustration.

10. Take his part against neighbors, teachers, policemen. They are all prejudiced against your child.

11. When he gets into real trouble, apologize for yourself saying, "I never could do anything with him."

12. Prepare for a life of grief. You will be likely to have it.

Parents of course should apply these twelve points just exactly in *reverse* to how they are given here. If done carefully and positively, healthy children will result from such treatment.

Children Learn What They Live

If a child lives with criticism, he learns to condemn.
If a child lives with hostility, he learns to fight.
If a child lives with fear, he learns to be apprehensive.
If a child lives with ridicule, he learns to be shy.
If a child lives with jealousy, he learns what envy is.
If a child lives with shame, he learns to feel guilty.
If a child lives with encouragement, he learns to be confident.
If a child lives with tolerance, he learns to be patient.
If a child lives with approval, he learns to accept himself.
If a child lives with recognition, he learns that it is good to have a goal.
If a child lives with sharing, he learns about generosity.
If a child lives with honesty, he learns what truth and justice are about.
If a child lives with security, he learns to have faith in himself and in those about him.
If a child lives with friendliness, he learns that the world is a nice place in which to live.
If you live with serenity, your child will live with peace of mind.

— Dorothy Law Nolte, in
The Lamplighter

The books listed on page 52 are recommended for parents to read as a means of helping to better establish their own and the family's love life. Parents cannot afford to risk damaging the lives of their children by their failures in this tremendously important area of life. [7]

Chapter 4

Problems of Parents

It is only logical that in this book problems should be dealt with which parents develop as a result of marriage. Every human institution has its flaws, and marriage is no exception. While we cannot anticipate all the problems of parents — and certainly each chapter deals with different aspects of parents' problems, we enumerate a few matters here which parents will do well to face. Some of the following suggestions are not so much "problems" as they are ways to *avoid* developing problems which parents inherit by having children. In every successful marriage, these matters need attention.

1. *Recognize the basic differences in each other and be prepared to accept them.* No two persons are alike in personality, including identical twins, who result from a split cell, making them as nearly a unit as possible. No two leaves in all the forests of earth are alike, and each individual is essentially different. The young couple newly married must accept this fact and live by this understanding if their marriage is to be a successful one. Their likes and dislikes may be made to blend nicely into each other's personality patterns if they try hard enough, but they will never be totally alike, no matter how hard they may try.

Once the couple accepts the totally different personality makeup each possesses, they can arrange to coordinate their affairs much better and come to a better understanding of each other, thereby finding more love and peace together. Failure to recognize and make these needed adjustments can only spell sorrow for them both, if not ultimate disaster.

[7] William Orr, *What Every Wife Should Know; What Every Husband Should Know;* O. A. Geiseman, *Make Yours a Happy Marriage;* Clyde M. Narramore, *Happiness in Marriage.*

2. *The man should be recognized as the head of the family,* if there is to be true peace and harmony. Mankind has not largely improved upon the old order of family life as first seen in the Bible. Scripturally, man is still the head of the family, and throughout the world society in general recognizes this factor. If there is to be a successful family framework, it must begin on this basis. The man must be a big enough man, in personality and development, to stand up, hitch his trousers, be a man, and head up the family.

Woman — the wife — was not taken from man's *head* in her original creation, signifying that she might dominate and rule her husband, nor from a bone in his foot, signifying that he might *trample* her. Rather, she was made from a "rib' out of his side, near the warm heart-pulsations of the throbbing center of life. She is to be his "help meet" — a word used in Genesis 2:20 which means literally, "a help sufficient." Look up the word "rib" and its meaning.

Dr. Edith Deen has said of woman and her place in the family:

> . . . the story of Adam and Eve . . . add vital concepts to the concept of marriage. . . . This early Bible story points to one of woman's important roles — that of helpmeet to her husband. Wives have rendered valuable help to their husbands in every field of human activity and in every period of the world's history from the time of Eve to the present. But woman was not created solely to be man's subordinate helper. . . . Created from the same substance as the man, woman was not inferior to him. [1]

The thesis is developed that while woman is subordinate to her husband in the legal sense, she is his equal in the moral, spiritual and social sense. Here she should stand by his side, sustaining and sometimes assisting in guiding him in life's masterful decisions.

If there is anything on earth that is fully detestable, it is to see a carping, crawling, spineless, whining, miserable male creature — I dare not call him a man! — who will not stand up and take his place in the home as the head of the family. I hasten to describe the position of proper "head" of the home. He is not a lord and master, with dictatorial powers, ruling with a rod of iron and browbeating his wife and children into silent subjection to his own selfish wishes and will. Nor is he a tyrant whose will is final authority and who without mercy demands unswerving obedience to his every command. Such a man is a *male beast,* but not a true loving husband and father.

On the contrary, the true husband and father and head of the home is a man of deep human understanding, true sympathies, and

[1] Edith Deen, *Family Living in the Bible,* pp. 4, 5.

the ability to see all sides of family situations. He must be a true lover of his wife and children. He is the bread winner and protector of the home and is also its spiritual leader. To be the proper head of the home, respected by the wife and children, he must take his place as the spiritual leader and adviser, standing tall and straight morally and socially, above reproach. He must be a person with ability to make moral judgments and proper decisions, as these will affect the family. The family must be able to turn in absolute confidence to him because of his personal integrity and piety.

Unfortunately, these demands immediately disqualify great hosts of men who would like to qualify, but spiritually, and many times otherwise, they are total "washouts." How can a spiritually minded wife and mother, whose biblical knowledge and intelligence about Christian matters supercedes that of her husband by about as much as a man does a mule, possibly turn to her husband for "guidance" in such matters? Perhaps he knows absolutely nothing about these matters and even swears at her when she dares to mention them to him. He will not even discuss them with her. Is she, then, to turn to him for guidance, sustenance, encouragement, enlightenment and help in those matters?

Someone asks, "But did not Paul tell the Corinthian women to keep silence in the church, and if they wanted to know anything of these matters, let them ask their husbands at home?" (Cf I Cor. 14:34, 35.) The reference here comes at the end of the passage about the matter of "confusion" in the church, which Paul is trying to straighten out. Clearly, he refers to the women babbling and talking out aloud in the public services, and not to their Christian ministries. And of course the passage refers to those Christian women who had Christian husbands who could explain to them at home what they wanted to know, and the regulation was for a local situation and not an order for the total Christian church. Let us be sensible here. What could a deeply spiritual wife who is well read in the Bible possibly learn from a spiritual ignoramus of a husband who is possibly a drunk, a moral washout, or a church fighter?

Certainly, the husband is ordained of God to be the head of the home, but that he is often not such a person is clearly evident. Even a ten-year-old child can see this. Man was created in God's image, but by sin he forfeited his place. Often a man forfeits his place as the true spiritual head of the home. Many times he becomes so totally indifferent through sinful practices which destroy him that he is not even capable of being the legal head of the home. Man must fit himself for every position he holds. The place of honor as the head of the home is earned by the man by his standard of conduct, not merely by his having been born a male and being married.

In many homes the true head of the home in any proper sense is the wife. She has fitted herself for the place of leadership, which the husband has totally disqualified himself for in every respect, except that he remains the male! No Christian woman anywhere wishes her husband to abdicate his place. All wives long for their husbands to take their place as the proper head of the home. In thousands of homes, if the wife and mother left all spiritual teaching, direction of children, moral and religious decisions and all such matters to an ungodly and disinterested husband, just *what* would the outcome be? Indeed, Paul said plainly, "I will therefore that younger women marry, bear children, *guide the house.* . . ." (I Tim. 5:14). These words, "guide the house," are full of significant meaning.

There is no other answer to Christian commitment and responsibility to God and the child-training which ungodly husbands have totally forfeited. The wife must carry it on. Otherwise, the children may be totally lost to Christ and His cause. I ask in solemn seriousness, which is the better thing for the wife to do? Let common sense and spiritual candor answer. In every way in which the man can and will accept his responsibility as head of the home, let him do so by all means.

3. *Do not reveal to each other the faults and sins of the past.* They are covered forever by the blood of Christ if the parents are Christians. If there has been misconduct on the part of either of the partners to a marriage, if they ever intend to reveal this fact, it should be done before marriage, preferably at the time of the engagement or shortly thereafter. Then, if either party is dissatisfied with the other, they can separate in peace and no harm will be done. But after the wedding day, the past should be sealed off safely and kept there forever. Even when the couple has been married as non-Christians and have kept certain information about misconduct before marriage a secret from each other, there seems to be no point in revealing it just because one has been converted to Christ. It is often detrimental to the happiness of both. *What good* can such a revelation now do either of them? It can never correct the past nor can it ever right it by any means. And there is not one single verse of New Testament Scripture which either demands or supports the notion that such matters should be confessed to each other.

A wife who made a mistake in her youthful life became a Christian. Under some kind of pressure she confessed to her husband all about this matter. He was not a Christian. He flew into a rage and told her he was leaving her if this was the kind of woman she was. The home disintegrated, and divorce followed. She accomplished nothing except the wrecking of their marriage. Had she kept still and worked with him, she might have won him to Christ and had a happy home. It never pays to drag pre-marriage skeletons out of the closet after marriage. "Let bygones be bygones," and let the couple build from their marriage onward a happy home together.

Little good can come, likewise, from telling unwholesome "family secrets." What good purpose can possbly be served? If there is no good purpose, why be telling about such things?

4. *Try to become adjusted to each other before the arrival of the first child.* Many methods are available for postponing the arrival of the first child; it is much better for the happiness of the couple and their home if there are no children for at least the first two years or so. The young couple need time for personal adjustments which must be made to each other first. Then, too, they need time for the full and complete satisfaction of the expressions of their own love for each other, undisturbed by any other factor. If they have had at least two years for these purposes before the first child is on its way, they can expect to be much better parents for the child.

Before marriage people tend to idealize each other, overlooking things that they do not agree upon. Sometimes they are not even aware of disagreement grounds. Because they are not sufficiently acquainted, often there is lack of full accord in many things. When these things come to light, a couple must work out a plan whereby they can "agree to disagree agreeably," if total agreement is impossible. Only on such a foundation can a successful marriage be built; otherwise it will "go sour" and possibly end in divorce. Adaptability is required in all human relationships. Marriage is no exception. This art must be learned; it is not natively acquired. People who have lived with roommates or in similar situations prior to marriage have learned, in part at least, the art of adjustment to other individuals, making the adjustment in marriage a bit easier.

Judson and Mary Landis are correct when they write:

> Most people who are in the early years of marriage today probably believe that the joys and satisfactions, and the frustrations and disappointments that they are experiencing in their married living are unique to themselves. . . . Many married people would probably become less disturbed by the frustrations and disillusionments that may occur at any stage of marriage if they knew how common in human experience are exactly the same situations that may distress them. They need to recognize that certain developmental tasks con-

front all married people. And these tasks are somewhat different at each of the four or five stages of the life cycle: (1) In early marriage; (2) when children come; (3) in middle life when the children leave home; (4) when retirement comes. (5) when crises occur such as death, serious illness, or financial disaster. [2]

Areas in which conflicts may arise and adjustments need be made are generally in sex relations, religion, social activities, recreation, in-law relationships, friendships.

The solving of conflicts, the Landis team points out, may be done in either of three ways:

> 1) Developing a relationship in which both compromise on all of the major points and determine to work them out as peacefully as possible. 2) If the couple find they hold seriously opposing views or discover they have antagonistic personality characteristics, they may learn to *accommodate* themselves to each other and make the best of it. They may reach a satisfactory compromise, agreeable to both, and each go his own way on these points. 3) They may develop a spirit of constant quarreling and bickering over differences, and remain in this state more or less for life. Or, they may learn to love each other enough to over-ride this; or failure here may bring an end to marriage. [3]

The *importance* of achieving adjustments in marriage is easily seen and should be done as early as possible in marriage. Adjustment is better late than never, but better sooner. The need is vital because of the effects on the marriage partners, the children who are born into the family, the relatives on each side, the general family life, the religious influence of each partner, the personal happiness of each of the pair.

The *time* element in adjustments is also imporant. Most "divorces occur within the first two or three years of marriage." Adjustments to each other may require years to make totally, yet the best of them ought to be well under way by the second year of marriage. The Landis' found in investigating four hundred married couples that more time was required to reach a complete adjustment in sexual relations and in the matter of spending the family income than in other fields of adjustments. These, then, may indicate the two hardest fields in which to achieve complete adjustment. Although about half the couples reported satisfactory adjustment in sex life from the beginning, some 47 percent said months or years had been required to achieve sexual adjustment, and some said it

[2] Judson Landis and Mary Landis, *Building a Successful Marriage,* p. 349.
[3] *Ibid.,* p. 354 - 356.

had never been reached. Family income and spending were about in the same ratio.

Landis and Landis also discovered in their investigations that the area in which fewest couples found complete adjustment was the *sexual* relationship. Their research bears out the report of the American Institute of Family Relations in Los Angeles, that 85 percent of all divorces are the result of a maladjustment in the sex relationships of the marriage partners. The area where the largest amount of satisfaction was achieved was in that of the friends of the married couples. There was no area for "fussing" here, and so here was found the highest peak of satisfactory achievement of pleasure.

Of the 409 couples, married between five and forty years, satisfactory adjustments in the seven major areas of life were as follows: sex relations, 63 percent; children, 71 percent; social activities, 72 percent; religion, 76 percent; spending family income, 77 percent; in-law relationships, 77 percent; mutual friends 82 percent.

Over 50 percent of these couples rated themselves as "very happy," about 35 percent as "happy," and 12 percent "average," if a good adjustment had been made from the beginning. If adjustment had taken from one to twelve months, the couples rated under the same scores as above, 50, 34, and 16 percent, respectively. Where between one and twenty years had been required for the adjustment, the couples rated under the same scores above, quite differently: 35, 44, 21; where there never had been a completely satisfactory adjustment, the ratings were: 19 percent, very happy; 35 percent, happy, and 46 percent average. These were the couples who had adjusted well in almost all areas, but had failed in two or three areas. It was assumed by the Landis' that when the couples did not adjust in more than three areas, divorce resulted and they were not included in these cases.

Helps in solving problems may be the following tension relievers: attend a social activity together; read a book; go for a swim, or a drive, together; or plan a love-making evening and follow it by wholesome intercourse. Nothing can be much more tension-relieving than this love-experience when at its best. God made people in such a manner that this is one of the most remarkable of all tension relievers.

Avoid quarrels over what someone has called "tremendous trifles" — little things over which husbands and wives often quarrel. Don't try too hard to remodel your mate — accept him or her — work slowly and ever so unnoticeably if you *must* do a remodeling job. Never do it before friends; and when you feel you have him about really remodeled, whatever you do, don't call attention to the success of your task in public!

Frequent attempts to test and prove the love of one's spouse are definite signs of immaturity. Neither party to a marriage should indulge in such activity. Jealousy, where there is no positive cause for it, is also a weakness arising out of the insecurity and fear of the jealous one that he does not have what it takes to possess and hold the other one. Untold grief has come from such utter senselessness! Jealousy never accomplished anything but to finally drive a wedge between the jealous partner and the other spouse. Jealousy is altogether unfounded unless one has evidence of unfaithfulness of the other partner. Marriage partners, to be completely happy, should *trust each other completely.* There should be a complete freedom of each one to talk with and have fun with other persons of the opposite sex without any questions as to their motives. Unless this is the case many a spouse feels bound, hedged in, uncomfortable and not trusted. These emotions in turn produce irritation and friction. Sometimes when persons are so jealous they cannot trust a mate out of sight, they indicate definite need for counseling. They may be suffering from a "persecution complex," known as *paranoia* — a form of emotional disorder. It is a senseless habit to be forever worrying about one's spouse.

5. *Sexual adjustment is one of the most important adjustments to be made in a marriage.* This adjustment is much easier for some couples than for others. It may require from a few days to several years, in some cases, to make a complete adjustment. Unfortunately, in a few cases it never is completely satisfactory, but in most cases there can be harmonious and blissful adjustment if both partners work at the task. If there appears to be difficulty in this adjustment, by all means see a counselor or your minister.

Sexual adjustment is one of the most delicate adjustments to be made, and time and patience are required for it to develop into the beautiful thing it should become. There are three phases of adjustment to be made here: 1. The biological adjustment, which has to do with organic factors. Here the help of a physician should be sought if there is any severe difficulty in the experience. 2. Often the lack of correct knowledge of the bodily organs and sexual factors is the cause for maladjustment. Wide reading about all these factors can greatly improve this phase. 3. Unfortunate social *conditioning,* especially on the wife's part, is often a great hindrance to her in making this adjustment.

The girl who has had no teaching from her parents about sex life often faces a serious drawback. Even worse, she may have had previous sex experience with someone else, or has been molested by some of her male relatives, for instance. A deep "guilt complex" has likely been set up if she has had premarital sex, along with a deep hostility toward the experience if there has been incest. Months of patient, tender care, love-making and wooing on the part of the husband may be required in such cases. It is best for a girl with any of these problems to seek help from a professional counselor. There is no need for embarrassment in any case; professional men have a complete knowledge in all these matters and know how to help one overcome bad *conditioning* and become a normal person. Going to a counselor is preferable to a couple trying to work out such problems alone, just as going to a doctor is better than trying to cure a disease on one's own.

With patience and love and cooperation by both parties, a harmonious adjustment can usually be made in a reasonable time.

Each one's mate needs the reassurance of love and tender care from time to time. This is a normal part of any healthy marriage. Failure at this point can become distressing for the one who needs love and care and does not receive it. To illustrate, there is the story of the newlyweds who moved into the house across the street from an older couple. One day the older wife noticed the young husband sitting with his wife on his lap as they showered affection on each other.

The older wife seeing the scene reported it to her husband who was reading his paper. She remarked, "John, I wish we had time to show a little affection for each other." He said nothing. Later she looked over the way and saw the couple sitting there. "John," she began in a wistful manner, "I can't even remember when you told me you loved me." That was too much for the old fellow.

Removing his glasses, and folding his paper, he came over to where she stood by the window. "Now, look, wife," he began in an air of importance, "when I married you, I told you I *loved you.* If I ever *change my mind,* I'll let you know!" He thought he had done her a most remarkable favor! It is too bad that many poor wives are married to such cold, heartless and unthoughtful men, but counseling reveals that this is too often the case. A man can put up no suitable argument in his defense for such cold-blooded treatment of a wife, for it is wrong by every standard of scriptural teaching (I Pet. 3:1-7; Eph. 5:22-33). And no wife has a Christian right to refuse to be cooperative in love-making and to be a normal sex partner to her husband, unless she is physically sick and unable to respond to him (I Cor. 7:5; I Pet. 3:1, 2). The word "conversation" in I Peter literally means "daily conduct." Many a husband has been driven to desperation and, finally, into the arms of another woman by the continual *frigidity* of his wife! Then she howls to the public how she is mistreated, when the fault is largely hers!

Many men drive their wives to frigidity by their thoughtlessness and carelessness in approaching them for lovemaking. I counseled a young divorcee recently who reported that her husband never "made love to her," warming her up and preparing her for the experience. Consequently, she never received anything from it. After he was asleep she would lie awake, desirous and unhappy. Finally, she left him in desperation and went with another man. This man made love to her, took plenty of time to prepare her for the sex act. She said, "For the *first time in my life, I learned that there could be pleasure in intercourse!* Then, I almost *hated* my husband for what he had done to me. I came back and we tried again, but, but it was the same old thing — he never seemed to understand. So, we separated and got a divorce." Of course she sinned, but whose fault was it? If it were not for the holding line of *morality* and for the sake of children, thousands of wives would not spend another night with their husbands! If one has been guilty here, he should quickly mend his ways!

The wife is usually the slower one to respond to sexual awakening and often needs much help from her husband to properly respond. If the husband is thoughtful, kind, and has studied how to help her achieve full response, her role as a sex partner is far happier. If the husband has never read anything about these matters nor sought help concerning them, he may be actually driving his wife to frigidity by his ignorance and crudity of his approach to her. The woman normally requires a far longer play period prior to the actual intercourse than does the man, because of both her biological and psychological needs. She is much different from the man in these needs, and unless her needs for "warming up" can be adequately met she will likely never receive the complete sense of satisfaction she needs from the experience.

Due to embarrassment, newness of the experience, and often the fact that the young bride has never been "awakened" sexually, she may require some time to actually receive any pleasure whatever from coitus. A young bride should not feel that she is abnormal or that something is wrong with her, therefore, if several weeks or even months elapse before she begins to enjoy the experience fully. Even among the more religious young people, petting has become so common that the average young bride has already been awakened and does not find it too difficult to respond to her husband in the early experience of sex. I have counseled with numbers of young men and their wives, however, who report that the wife seldom reaches a complete climax in intercourse.

There may be several reasons for the above; including, first, the newness of the experience to the young wife and her need for better psychological preparation for it. Second is the youthfulness on her part, especially if she is only in her early twenties or younger. Normally, the woman does not reach her highest peak of sexual desire until between twenty-two and twenty-eight and up to thirty-five sometimes, whereas the average boy reaches his peak of both desire and activity at from eighteen to about twenty-five. He then levels off at about this peak and holds it until the late forties or early fifties. This lateness of reaching peak desire may be a hindrance to the young wife in climaxing properly.

Third is the fact that often the husband does not properly prepare his wife for the experience. There needs to be a "play period" of intense love-making, petting and fondling and playing with the various female organs to arouse proper passion in many wives. This period may need to extend from ten to as much as forty-five minutes or more at times, before the actual intercourse begins. Often husbands rush through their part of the experience as if they were going to a fire, leaving the poor wife only partially warmed up, not even ready for the experience when they are through. The husband will then go to sleep immediately, leaving his wife lying awake with an aroused passion and no way to be properly satisfied. Such treatment by husbands is not uncommon. Many wives report it in counseling sessions. It is one of their biggest "gripes" against their husbands.

One young wife in desperation exclaimed to me in a counseling session, "He could get anything on earth he wants from me, if he only had sense enough to love me a little at some *other* time than then!" She was desperate. Her husband, a busy minister, did not *intend* to be cold toward her, but he was, just the same. The largest complaint of most wives against their husbands is this very thing — the husband seldom shows any affection or concern *except* when he wants something for himself. How utterly *selfish* and thoughtless some men can be is almost unbelievable! One wife complained, "I can hardly stand for him to touch me! I know exactly what he wants when he comes around trying to be loving. He *never* shows a solitary concern or expression of affection at *any* other time." Can you honestly blame her? Men, wake up and realize that a wife wants to be loved, petted, told she is pretty and made over when she *knows* you have no sexual purpose in the show of affection. Any husband should know this, but apparently many do not, or at least, do not practice it if they do. It is a sad commentary on manly love.

About twenty-five to thirty-five percent of American wives are reported to be frigid — that is, they receive little or no pleasure from coitus and seldom or never reach a climax. Doctors and psychiatrists believe that this problem is more psychological than biological. If the women had loving and tender husbands who had from the beginning properly loved and given them the needed "fore-play," they would have developed out of this state into naturally warm wives who would enjoy the experience.

I recall a case of a wife of about thirty-five who in her some fourteen years of marriage had climaxed only once or twice. A thorough medical examination assured her nothing was wrong. Her doctor advised her that the problem was largely psychological. We began counseling toward helping her to overcome the psychological blockage which had largely brought about the condition. Her Christian husband, who, when he understood more of her condition after being counseled also, did his best to help her. After we had cleared up the "guilt complex" resulting from unfortunate girlhood experiences with sex — often a major factor in the frigidity of wives — she began to improve. After about a year of counseling she was able to achieve complete climaxes. Her joy knew almost no bounds. But without professional help she would probably have lived out her life without reaching this wonderful experience.

It is not necessary for a wife to climax every time there is intercourse. Sometimes the experience of satisfying her husband and of herself reaching a certain amount of satisfaction is perfectly satisfying and she needs nothing more. It is a golden ideal when wife and husband can climax *together*, but if this ideal is reached once out of three times on an average, it is very satisfactory indeed. The wife is usually the slower one. The husband should stay with her and help her to completion if she wishes to climax.

In some cases the wife almost never climaxes without special help from the husband. Sometimes she can only do so when her clitoris is massaged, either by the husband's penis or manually. In such a case, the husband should help the wife, either before or after his own climax. Occasionally, too, the husband will have difficulty. Often he climaxes far too early to receive much satisfaction from the experience. In such a case, he could find it helpful to get his mind on something else during the early part of the experience. Sometimes, too, he has a certain ailment which needs medical attention, and he should seek a doctor's help. After the age of fifty or so, he may find it taking much longer to reach a climax. Often the reason is that the act occurs too often. In these cases he may need to regulate the act to fewer times with longer spaces between, or to improve his psychological conditioning by a change of his thought patterns during the experience. If his problem continues long, he will wish to seek a physician's aid.

Researchers have found that there is a wide swing of practice in the frequency of coitus. Some couples report a range from once a night, when younger, to once a year in older years. Even in early years some couples do not desire marital relations often. Reports show the average frequency of couples from twenty to thirty years of age about seven times per month, while those who are from fifty to sixty years of age decrease to about three times a month. From ages thirty to fifty there is a great variation, but a reasonable normalcy would perhaps be from about three times per week in the younger bracket to once a week or ten days in the older age bracket. [4]

A British social scientist who has done considerable work in this field recently reported that with good health and a normal practice of sexual life, a man may continue to enjoy this experience until in his nineties! My own counseling ministry has proved this fact. One man in his late sixties reported enjoying this experience every night without in any way impairing himself. Another man of eighty reported having difficulty because his wife was not cooperative enough to meet his needs.

On the other hand, there are wives, especially, and occasionally husbands, who had intercourse so frequently in their early years that all desire was destroyed. This is especially true of women who were pressed into relations by their husbands more frequently than they desired, and who were turned against sex entirely. Usually the difficulty here is psychological, not biological. Often overweight women, also, after they pass age thirty-five or forty, or even at younger ages, have little or no desire for the experience. Possibly the excessive weight, tiring them out and leaving them exhausted by day's end has much to do with the problem. Some few men are totally impotent by age fifty or sixty. These are rare cases, usually, and are caused by either physical difficulty or psychological blockage. [5]

Another strange phenomenon is that quite often after menopause women who have previously been only mildly interested in sex or

4 *Ibid.*
5 *Ibid.*, p.393.

even frigid will become exceptionally passionate. Such may be the case when older women — widows or divorcees — are out avidly seeking men. Now that the use of the pill has become common, and the fear of pregnancy has largely disappeared, many women who were before much less desirous are now much warmer and more passionate. This change is of course understandable and may be to some extent a partial explanation of why after menopause some women have a far deeper interest in sex.

6. *Live a normal sex life.* By the time marriage partners have reached mid-life, if there is a considerable family, they are often so involved with work and social life that many times their own sex life is seriously affected. By day's end the grind of work, the round of parties, the social engagements, the home activities, *ad infinitum*, have so drained them that they are almost washed out. Late to bed, both worn out, they either seldom engage in this most wonderful experience, or if so, "get it over in a hurry," so they can get to sleep. This latter utterly destroys all the tenderness and love of the experience and makes it distasteful, especially to the wife.

When a couple fail to make love and have normal sex life, their marriage is likely to slowly descend from the high plateau of happiness and bliss it should be lived on to the barren plains of coldness, or the swamps and bogs of quarreling and picking at each other. There are many marriages which have been blissful in former years which come to a stalemate with the partners bickering, shouting at each other, and showing coldness toward each other. This is pitiable. The children are disillusioned with marriage, and the smaller ones deeply hurt emotionally, being slowly developed into future cases of frustration, emotional disturbance and possible ill health, and in a few cases, to mental disorder which will require severe treatment to cure. And yet, all could be avoided if the parents are determined to keep a normal love and sex life intact and if they have been the kind of partners they should have been in life.

Statistics have revealed that the middle period of life can often be one of the richest and most enjoyable for husband and wife as sex partners. The deep meanings which come to be attached to the experience, the calm and utter bliss of it, the way in which it may be prolonged into a most enjoyable time, are all favorable to this period of life as possibly the very most enjoyable time of the entire marriage. There should now be more time for each other and better circumstances under which to enjoy each other. This form of life should then take on the richness and color of the most extreme blessedness of the whole marriage up to this time.

If marriage partners are temperate and sensible in their approach to sex life in younger years, it may be enjoyed until the very sunset years.

7. *Religion sometimes constitutes a problem for parents in the home.* There is the matter of the family altar. Sometimes ungodly husbands object to having prayer of any kind with the children. In such cases the wife is not bound to conduct family prayers, if the husband refuses to allow her to do so. However, since the home is just as much hers as his, she has the right, also, to disobey his orders and conduct prayers with her children if she feels this to be her duty. There are times when to do the right thing means defying certain orders which are contrary to God's higher law, which takes precedence over man-made laws. The three Hebrew children went into the furnace of fire for disobedience to a senseless royal decree which had been enacted to scare them out of fulfilling their duty to God. If nothing more, the Christian wife certainly has the obligation to pray with and teach her children the Christian way.

Religion has its place in every home and is needed to bring complete happiness and stability to the home. Statistics show the following interesting facts about the effects of religion and home life on divorce, for instance. The Catholic Church has fewer divorces than any other ethnic group, while the Jewish people follow with the next lowest figures. Of a study of 6,000 families, divorce shows only 3.8 percent for Catholics; 10 percent for Protestants; 17 percent for mixed between Protestant and Catholics; 23.9 percent among those with no religion. Similar studies are found to reveal almost the same results. [6] It is safe to say, then, that lack of any religion in the family produces the highest divorce rate of any situation.

Landis and wife found the following relationship between religion and married happiness in the home. Devoutly religious groups reported 47 percent *very* happy; 33 percent happy, with only 20 percent average or unhappy in their marriages. Of the slightly religious groups, only 38 percent were very happy; 30 percent were happy; 32 percent said they were average or unhappy. The non-religious groups reported only 21 percent being very happy; 28 percent happy; while 51 percent reported being average or unhappy with their marriages. It is evident that most married happiness can be expected in homes where active religious faith is practiced.

In cases of *total agreement* in religious beliefs, 65 percent reported being very happy, as against only 33 percent reporting happiness where there was disharmony in religious beliefs. Of interest

[6] *Ibid.*, pp. 243, 244.

was the fact that almost 80 percent of marriages occurring in parsonages and churches revealed a far better marital adjustment than marriages in the home or in civil ceremonies. [7] This was not necessarily because the weddings occurred in churches or parsonages, but rather because the participants in such weddings were largely from Christian homes where Christian partners set up the new home, whereas the others were non-Christian. Statistically, Christianity in the home beats the record for happiness in marriage, as over against non-Christian marriages.

Religious experience provides for the individual a sense of security and stability of personality which cannot be found aside from it. It gives emotional balance and ability to rise over life's changing vicissitudes; it brings balance in the crisis hours of life which the non-Christian does not have. Recourse to the Bible for comfort is of supreme importance in times of testing and trouble, which are sure to come to all homes sooner or later.

Christianity is a religion of spiritual and moral values and is not dependent upon material successes or possessions for its success in meeting life's crises. Its values are based on more solid and enduring foundations than material things can ever afford. There is also a vast difference between the valid Christian whose life is lived in keeping with the teaching of Christ and the New Testament, and the one who merely makes a profession of religion or holds to some religious dogma, without much true Christian commitment being attached to his religious life.

True spiritual devotion gives ability to succeed with proper Christian self-discipline — a necessity for complete happiness in any successful marriage. It also provides the ability to refrain from nagging, accusing and other evil habits which non-Christians often fall into. Thus, there is more happiness in the home where there is true faith.

Parents need religious experience to help them to do their best with their children. No amount of moralizing and good training can ever take the place of devout Christian living on the part of the parents. The best example is the Christian example. It will teach the children more and do it more effectively than anything else in the world. "Example is stronger than precept," said a great man long ago. Then he thought a moment and exclaimed, "Example is ten times stronger than precept!"

An excellent book for Christian parents is *The Christian Family*, edited by Roy W. Howell, and published by Light and Life Press,

[7] *Ibid.*, pp. 430 - 434.

Winona Lake, Indiana. It has much helpful material which will be of service in developing the many-sided interests of the Christian home.

8. *Parents should not contradict each other in child-correction.* Parents should agree never to disagree on a child's correction *before the child.* If they wish to disagree about the manner or amount of punishment meted out, they should wait until they are alone.

Sometimes when one of the mates is not a Christian, a problem is created. The mother, for instance, wants to forbid the child to do certain things which she feels are not in his best interest. But the father immediately defends the child against his mother, saying, "Ah, nonsense; let him go ahead — I see no harm in this!" Immediately, the mother is down-graded before the child, who then becomes confused by the double standard. Often, too, he takes delight in the division of the parents from which he usually benefits temporarily. However, he may suffer loss in the long run. [8]

9. *Should the mother work away from home?* For centuries the mother was never away from her home and children for very long periods of time. Home was her domain and she was the queen there. In those times babes and young children had their needs for love and care adequately met, and neurotic young people and adults with personality and mental problems were fewer than they are today. Criminality, too, was far below the level of percentage that it is today.

The Industrial Revolution changed the old ways, however. Now many mothers work away from home. In far too many instances the mother bears the child and is soon back to work away from home. The baby has a baby-sitter who cares about as much for him as she does the average cat — not nearly so much as for her *own cat!* The child thus is robbed of the tender loving care he so much needs. Dr. Ernest Shelley, Treatment Supervisor for Michigan State Correctional Department, once said, "For every young person that I have seen damaged by 'smother love,' I have seen two hundred hurt by not enough love." [9] The theory of some years ago that babies should be left strictly alone, and not "smothered by love," has been proved to be false and dangerous. In those periods of earth's history when people had the best of emotional and mental health as adults, at the same time they had the most attention and mother-father and family love in childhood.

[8] Wm. S. Deal, *A Happy Married Life and How to Live It*, chap., "Be Comrades in a Common Cause."

[9] Roy W. Howell, *The Christian Home*, p. 4.

Because of the impossibility of the mother paying proper attention to her children while working away from home, one could raise the serious question whether it is right for her to do so. The cost in the end may far outweigh the gains made by her income. If she can arrange to do work within the home so that she can give the needed attention to the children, this may be fine. But rearing a family properly and keeping a household going is a full time job. If people were willing to live more nearly within an ordinary income and did not demand so many of the extras of life, mothers would not need to work out away from home. If the present awful crime rate is partly the result of so many baby-sitter-reared children, we must face up to the frightful possibilities of what a mother's work may do to her children. Shaw and Johnson, who made many investigations of family life, felt definitely that for the best interest of her children and family the mother should not work away from home. [10] Their investigation seemed to reveal it was detrimental to the child's welfare and future behavior for the mother to be absent from him during his tender years.

10. *Find time to be together alone as parents.* Many parents find almost no time for each other after the second or third child arrives. The whole realm of time and home activities is child-centered, and the parents are almost never together alone, except when they retire at night. Often the bedroom door is swung open without a knock or warning, and a child bursts in with some complaint or request. Some parents put locks on their bedroom doors to avoid such unceremonious intrusions, while others feel this would be an affront to the children, setting up all kinds of questions as to *why* the door is locked. In this case, simply explain to them, "This is mother's and daddy's bedroom, and no one is to come into this room after we retire without knocking and asking permission." After all, parents can stand to be treated with a little common courtesy, even by their own children. And children should be taught the need to be courteous, even to parents!

Find time for an evening out together alone as in the good old days of courtship or early marriage. Parents need this diversion to give them some emotional freedom from the grinds of life, as well as to talk over many things which concern them and the family. There are often things which need their attention alone. The price of a baby-sitter is not too much to pay now and then for an evening out. A man should take his wife out to dinner now and then, as relief from the constant grind with which she has to live. After

[10] Doreen Shaw and Bertha Johnson, *Your Children,* pp. 127 ff.

dinner, why not go for a drive and park somewhere and enjoy an hour together? If this sort of thing has lost its appeal, either you are getting very old or your marriage could stand a little mending work done on it!

Another thing needful in making adjustments is that each partner must not expect the other to accept his role of life concepts about things. Each one has his own way of doing things. Why try to change him? You only hamper and distract him and make him feel that you do not really accept him. Truthfully, there are many spouses who do *not* accept their mates. They really *want to change them*. If you want to change your mate, you should do so *before* marriage rather than trying it afterwards. It hurts a mate to feel that his or her ways are rejected by the other. Some men never seem to tire of telling how superior they are to their wives, or how much better their mothers did things than their wives do. You liked your mother's way better, why not *stay with your mother?* But now that you are married, it is time you *grew up* and *became a man,* and stopped breaking your wife's heart by everlastingly bringing up such matters. On the other hand, nothing is much more galling to a man than a constantly *nagging* wife. Some men do little that is ever *right;* there has to be some complaint.

Some women appear to have been born in "Nag's Hollow" and have never gotten out of it. Even if the man is not faultless in his manners, and in other small matters, let him alone. Give him a bit of encouragement now and then. At the least sign of any improvement, praise him generously, and you will accomplish far more. Many a man has been driven away from home by nothing more than a nagging wife. The writer of Proverbs said, "It is better to dwell in a corner of the housetop, than with a brawling woman in a wide house" (Prov. 21:9). Another rendering refers to the "brawling woman in a wide house" as a "woman of contentions," and the "wide house" as a "house of society." The eastern people built flat houses, and often the roof was used for a "porch" or even a summer dwelling. It was usually a quiet place away from the noise of the household. Is it any wonder some men seek the quiet of being "away from home" until late hours at night?

There are many problems which parents will run into along the way, but these are some of the more extreme ones. There are no problems which a pair cannot solve by patiently and cooperatively working together.

The following lines, representing a child's plea to his parents, are apt and should be studied carefully by parents.

DEAR MOM AND DAD

1. *Don't spoil me.* I know quite well that I ought not to have all I ask for. I am only testing you.

2. *Don't be afraid to be firm with me.* I prefer it. It makes me feel more secure.

3. *Don't let me form bad habits.* I have to rely on you to detect them in the early stages.

4. *Don't make me feel smaller than I am.* It only makes me behave stupidly "big."

5. *Don't correct me in front of people if you can avoid it.* I'll take much more notice if you talk quietly with me in private.

6. *Don't protect me from consequences.* I need to learn the painful way sometimes.

7. *Don't take too much notice of my small ailments.* I am quite capable of trading on them.

8. *Don't nag.* If you do, I shall have to protect myself by appearing deaf.

9. *Don't make rash promises.* Remember that I feel badly let down when promises are broken.

10. *Don't forget that I cannot explain myself as well as I should like.* That is why I am not always very accurate.

11. *Don't be inconsistent.* That completely confuses me and makes me lose faith in you.

12. *Don't put me off when I ask questions.* If you do you will find I will stop asking and seek my information elsewhere.

13. *Don't tell me my fears are silly.* They are terribly real, and you can do much to reassure me if you try to understand.

— From On and Off Duty

Chapter 5

Family Framework

The family is a unit. It was ordained of God as the mainspring of society; it has endured as such ever since. It is a necessary social structure for the well-being of the individual. People, like the great redwood trees of northern California, grow best not as individuals like the average tree, but as units. Often in this great forest one will see two to five redwood trees growing almost as if together, as a unit. The individual who is healthiest emotionally is the person who grows up in a loving family relationship. Societies which have tried to destroy the family unit have failed in every case. Even in modern Russia the communal idea failed and in order to preserve the nation it was necessary to revert to the family idea. One cannot go against what God has founded in nature and prosper.

In the family unit there must be certain structural and cultural orders. The parents present the apex and the children make up the completed structure, out of which the family framework arises. There must then emerge certain standards of conduct, rules, and regulations; cultural and social situations develop as a result of these. Each family ultimately develops certain things as its particular "mores" and "folkways," or patterns. For instance, in certain families it becomes the standard rule that each member has certain chores to do daily as his part of the family work. This is a structured social situation. Out of it arises a cultural pattern which may give to the child certain life-long benefits. Just as this is true of this one simple situation, so it it true of the many more situations which develop within the family.

Out of this unit of structured life develops what might be termed multi-phased situations. These in turn must each be dealt with as need demands. Some of these situations are good, some are bad or may be harmful, but they cannot well be avoided; however, they can be dealt with successfully.

The family unit is held together by love and common interests. Within this structure there should be a sort of 'framework" within which family members operate. If it is built into a strong structure, it can withstand every onslaught of the enemies of family life.

Since man was first upon the earth, mankind has had families. The home is the oldest institution known to man and the most lasting. It preceded the church and, of course, human government. Possibly the idea of government over men at large arose out of the simple rules governing the ancient tribe, which in turn came from the structure of the family.

Sometimes children imagine it would be a most glorious thing if there were no *rules* to be kept in the family. Just let everyone do as he pleases and oh, what fun we would have! Well, let's see about this. This means that if William, the oldest boy wishes to use anything in the home, including *my things,* he has perfect liberty to do so. If the youngest child wants to bang on the piano until no one can hear anything else, that's fine; and if the parents wish to eat all the food on the table, before the children are up, and there is none left for the children, hurrah for the parents! "Oh, yeah, I see — that wouldn't work very well, would it?" I thought you'd see by this little example how necessary just a few rules in the family really are!

The family life is structured, then, by the fact of *absolute need* for this framework. Suppose you just try for one or two days allowing everyone to do as he pleases with no kind of order whatsoever, and see what results. It may take several days to get things back into any decent order. Here are a few simple factors which may help the average family work out a better program of living.

1. *The family forum.* Some families have found this worked exceptionally well. By the "forum" we mean a weekly meeting of the family when major things of interest to the whole family are discussed, or other things settled. There are many such things which may be profitably discussed. It may not be a bad idea, in homes where there are two or more children who are past eight or ten, to make some standard rules about corrections for wrongdoing. Perhaps the children will help to formulate some rules as to what should be done in cases of disobedience, misbehavior, stealing, or lying, for instance. We agree, for instance, that if Bill lies about something this means a certain type of punishment; and if Susie takes something which is not hers, another type of punishment is decreed.

We may discuss the coming family outing, or the vacation that is coming up; each contributes his ideas as to what and how to make it a success. Or, maybe it's the spring or fall trip to visit relatives, and all of us make our contribution to the plans.

In this way the work for the week may also be laid out and each one assigned his chores, or special plans may be made for something unusual which is to take place in the home or community. There are many things which the weekly or even monthly forum could help to care for.

Of course, the forum idea may not be as popular now as in the days of the larger family. However, even with two or three children it may be worked successfully. Blood and Wolfe questioned hundreds of housewives in their survey, made in the Detroit, Michigan, general area, both in the city and on farms, as to how many children they thought would be an ideal family. "Ninety-three percent of the city wives and almost as many farm wives answered between two and four." [1] So, today's families are generally smaller, but even here the family forum may be made effective.

2. *The family altar.* For long years the family altar has been a Christian institution. In the later years the many intrusions into family life, such as the many recreational attractions, school classes, and other activities at night, have quite largely dissected the family. When it is small and beginning, the parents can have a more successful family altar than when the children grow up and yet remain in the home during late high school years. Nevertheless, it pays to keep up the family altar, even when to do so requires sacrifice. Edith Deen has well said on this point: "One of Israel's greatest sources of strength was its worship of God by the entire family (Deut. 16). Israel's families felt God's greatness yet nearness, His holiness and His Presence. . . . These primitive people bear a striking contrast to many of today's families, who have no time for worship together, and consequently walk toward many dangers." [2]

The strength of the family is its unity; and this unity cannot be strengthened any more than by the solemn family altar worship of the entire membership as a family unit. It is true that the "families that *pray* together *stay* together," today just as in older times. Our national strength will never rise above our family strength; our family strength depends almost entirely upon the religious fabric and moral support which comes from it. A democracy

[1] R. O. Blood and D. M. Wolfe, *Husbands and Wives, the Dynamic of Married Living*, pp. 118, 119.

[2] Edith Deen, *Family Living in the Bible*, p. 143.

cannot long survive the breakdown in its family life. Democracies are built upon the honor, honesty, integrity and confidence of the individuals who compose them. When household religion goes out the family window, some other form of government, usurping the rights and privileges of the individual, is ready to fly into the national political window and take over the reins of leadership.

Concerning the place of love in family life Edith Deen observed:

> The family at its best is a nursery of love. This natural aspect of a family is perhaps its highest reason for being. To begin life as one who is loved and grow up surrounded by the warmth and tenderness of family affection is to be supremely fortunate. Love flourishes in a happy home where parents, children, sisters, brothers, wives, and husbands care for each other and express affectionate interest in the well being of all. [3]

Edith Deen has expressed the sources of family unity in ancient Israel as love of country, obedience to law, faith in the destiny of God's people, faith in God and a knowledge of the Scriptures. [4] These same principles are a groundwork for true family unity and strength in our own times.

What does all this have to do with the family altar? Just this: There is no other place nor time than at the family altar whereby these virtues so important to holding the family together can better be instilled into the children, and strength and guidance be received for the parents for this task. There is a special source of strength which comes from the banding of a family together around the family altar time which nothing else can give to it. This special season of "home worship" is as important in its place in the home as is the season of weekly church worship to the community at large.

Unfortunately, in some instances the family worship time has been misconducted to its detriment. To wait until the children are ready for bed is the common practice in many instances. Sometimes the younger ones are asleep or very sleepy; the older ones are sometimes absent from the home, and the worship period is ineffective. Would it not be much better to reserve the time for this service just after the evening meal, when everyone is there? If this time is chosen, then the family must be taught that each one must be there for this occasion. There will be no excusing certain ones to go on their way to some engagement, leaving the family circle muti-

[3] *Ibid.*, p.158.
[4] *Ibid.*, 163 - 166.

lated. The evening meal will be served early enough for all to attend this important service.

Some families have found that it is better to have this period just following breakfast. In this case the whole family arises fifteen to thirty minutes early so there is plenty of time before school or work hours. This rule becomes standard and no one would think of not being there unless he is sick in bed. I have observed this rule in operation and believe it to be a fine time for such family worship, before the day begins. Each family will need to select a time most suitable and then hold each member to it.

This service should be brief and to the point, not a time to wear everyone out by long Scripture lessons, exhortations, or long, rambling prayers for all the work of God over the world. If Scripture is read, it should be brief with any comments to the point. In a larger family, allow one or two children each day to pray, until each has prayed his turn, then the parents in their turn. In this way the service can be kept brief, interesting and appealing. It can easily become dead and meaningless, but it can also be made one of the most interesting times of the day!

If the father is not a Christian, then the mother should conduct this service. If the mother is not a Christian and there is a younger member of the family who wishes to do so, then he or she should read and pray with the rest of the family.

If it is found impractical to have family worship daily, then it should be done on a weekly basis, on Saturday or Sunday, or whenever is the best time for the family. Family altar once a week well done is better than a poorly conducted service daily. It may come in time to mean more to the children, but it should in no case be neglected.

3. *Tensions of family life.* It is almost impossible to live in such close connections as a family must live without tensions developing now and then. There are times when the parents will be tense and frustrated by the constant grinds of life. Sometimes under such tensions they may even become a bit irritable. When this occurs each should know that he is pressing his work or home activities too hard and should relax and get hold of himself. Children are often irritable and make for unhappiness in relationships by giving vent to their tensions.

When the tensions are running a bit high in the family it is a good time to take off a few minutes and have a game of some kind, if possible. Or, try in some way to lessen the tensions by demanding that the children get possession of their emotions and stop yelling at each other. Sometimes, too, if there is music in the home, it can be played to soften the tensions. At any rate, try to keep the tensions from erupting into yelling sessions or fighting among the children. A certain amount of brother-sister rivalry is natural and normal, but when it reaches a crest point, it is time for relaxing it in some definite way.

Brother-sister tensions and sharp words are a common lot of the larger family life. They are nothing to be alarmed about except when these conditions continue day after day, with the spear and sword continuously thrust at certain members of the family. Animosity or hostility could develop which could hurt one or more of the children deeply, emotionally; sometimes years are required for someone to get over family feuds which are allowed to develop far in excess of what is healthy and normal. When a situation develops between any two definite members of the family in which the hostility becomes a fixed thing and is regularly manifested toward a definite member of the family, the parents need to act, for such a problem can develop into something serious. There may be good psychological reasons for the hostility and if so, immediate attention should be given to those involved in it.

Parent-child tensions also often develop. These are usually harmless. Girls who have been ardent admirers and lovers of their dads often develop a hands-off policy toward them when they enter the early teen years. This is the effect of the change toward the boy-girl relationship. Sometimes the girl wants to attract boys and feels that if her father shows her affection she will still appear the little girl type, and she is so anxious to *grow up* that she wants her father to leave her completely alone. In this way she feels grown up. A few girls develop quite early, sex feelings which disturb them when a man hugs or shows affection to them, and for this reason they shy away from their fathers. Sometimes, too, at this age the girl takes a belligerent attitude toward her father for some unknown reason — usually as unknown to her as to the parents. Often about this time, too, there develops the eternal mother-daughter hassle. It has gone on since Eve's first daughters took issue with her, and it will not likely stop. One has to simply learn how to cope with this situation and make the best of it.

Sometimes, too, boys become belligerent toward their father in the mid-teen period, especially if a strong-willed boy feels that his father is too strict with him. He has a mistaken notion of where final authority lies. The lad has reached the place where he may earn as much as his dad, or is as strong physically, so in some way he begins to compare his prowess with that of his father. Fathers do well to largely ignore this attitude and try to get along the best they can with their rebellious sons. Often an understanding father can sit down and talk with his son and come to some reasonable terms. A truly understanding father can in this way often discover the basis for his son's hostility and can help the boy face up to the real problem which is making him act rebellious.

Instead of taking stern measures with him, find out first what is behind his behavior. Sometimes misunderstanding, personal feelings of inadequacy, deep guilt feelings arising from a misunderstanding of some of his natural boy problems, or other things could be the reason for the sudden change of behavior. One needs to understand that his own children also have their problems which need to be faced up to and adequately dealt with if the young person is to be saved from suffering either deep emotional problems or maybe turning to more violent forms of behavior as a means of trying to deal with his problems.

4. *Work for all the family.* Aside from worship, there is no more worthy activity in which one can engage than work. Before Adam sinned in his Edenic paradise God put him into "the garden of Eden to dress and keep it" (Gen. 2:15). Man was ordered to work, therefore, before sin ever entered this world. And it is most likely that had man never sinned he would have had pleasant work to do for his betterment.

Work for each member of the family is both healthy and helpful. Each one should have an assigned task, be it ever so small. Even small children are often joyous when they have some small work suited to them to perform. It is not good for children to be idle. It is too true as Ben Franklin once said, "Satan finds some mischief still for idle hands to do."

Therefore, every child should be taught to do his share of the work. Each should keep his room or share in keeping it clean and in order. If the home tasks are arranged for properly, the mother can have several pleasant hours a day for needful types of work other than household drudgeries.

> Every child must be taught to work. Work is valuable — (*Family Framework*). All growing young people need activity and there are many other values to work than mere physical ones, great as these are: There are *educative* values. We learn by doing. Work teaches industry, initiative, success, love of values, and many other worthwhile lessons. Some of the greatest early industrialists of this nation came

from farms where they had learned as children to work. Check in *Britannica* stories of Ford, Woolworth, Morgan, Schwab, McCormick, Elisha Howe, Edison, Hoover, MacArthur, Eisenhower, Rockefeller, and see how many of these men were hard working boys.

Work teaches *moral* values, such as character, truthfulness and the valueability to stick to a thing till it is finished. Never allow a child or young person to start things without finishing them . . . Make Mary finish the dress she starts; or John, the old car he starts to re-vamp, etc . . . If not, they will pay later by their being unable to carry through in more important things. Mary comes bringing her baby, sobbing, "I can't take it any longer — I've come home." Her marriage folds — she never learned to carry through what she started. John, the same, or he never keeps a job long enough to go to the top . . . no persistence; never taught it at home; doesn't know *how!*

Someone has well said, "The devil tempts other men, but idle men tempt the devil." Henry Drummond once remarked, "God gave us work, not so much because the world needs it, but because the worker needs it. Men make work, but work makes men." [5]

Many of the great men of our nation of the recent past did such things as sell papers, deliver groceries, and run errands. In years past when a bank wanted to develop a future executive, a promising boy was often hired as an errand boy. More and more responsibility was entrusted to him. Sometimes he was started off with small sums of money which he could have pilfered, to try him out. If he proved trustworthy, larger sums were sent by him. Later, he was given other work in the bank; and it has been said that many a successful bank president was once an errand boy! A good personal friend of mine since boyhood days is now the manager of the Duke University Bookstore, Durham, North Carolina. He worked his way through the University selling papers. Generally, young people who work their way through college are more successful than those whose way is paid by wealthy parents or others. Work does something for one which nothing else can do.

5. *Family recreation.* Recreation is more necessary in our society than it was fifty years ago. We are more sedentary and therefore in need of more man-made devices for recreation. Commercial recreation is now popular, but its weakness is that we are becoming a nation of "spectators" who partake of less and less of the recreation so necessary for our own physical and social betterment.

The home can be a place of many-sided recreations with just a

[5] Clarence H. Benson, *An Introduction to Child Study*, pp. 126, 127.

little imagination and work on the part of the parents and the older young people. All the family should be encouraged to have fun at home. It would be well to organize a "have fun at home" night once a week at least. Today, the older young people are gone to every form of outside activity almost every night or they are brooding over the fact that they are so "pent up and shut out" of life's activities. Even if they are restricted at home for only a night or two per week, some of them howl as if half of their life had suddenly fallen away! This reaction is unhealthy morally, socially and spiritually, to say nothing of the physical drain often imposed upon the young people.

An evening at home with many sorts of games, when guests of the children's ages will be invited, can be plenty of fun. The home should provide record players, musical instruments of whatever kind the children can play, and other means of entertainment. If the home is not large enough, and there are several children, let them set to work to enlarge it by digging a basement if this is possible or building on a recreation room. It is amazing what an interested family can do to make the home a really entertaining and attractive place for themselves and others. Good books for those who love reading should be provided and the children's rooms should be cared for in a manner to make them attractive.

A happy family life can be made if all try hard to cooperate in it. For instance, each birthday should be made an occasion for a birthday dinner, with a cake and candles, gifts, and fun. Maybe, too, a friend of the age of the one having the birthday may be invited. Every holiday should also be celebrated with all the trimmings, and the story of the day told to the children at the special dinner or at an appropriate time. Trips to the mountains, the ocean, lakes, museums, parks and other such places should be planned, along with other outings which will afford the children pleasure and information. One should plan to attend camp meetings, youth conferences and camps, and many other religious events to give the child experience with religious activities, thereby generously exposing him to the opportunity for personal involvement not only in the activities, but most important of all, personal involvement and commitment to the Christ about whom these activities center.

6. *An allowance for each child.* Not all parents agree with the policy of giving an allowance for each child. If allowances are not given, then some form of policy whereby the children are allowed to make or secure money is needful. Practically the same rules should apply to money regardless of how it comes to the child.

If the allowance is given it may be either weekly or monthly; however, a child has difficulty in waiting a whole month for his allowance, and possibly the weekly plan is best.

Children should be taught to pay tithes on their income and so honor the Lord with their money as well as with their lives. They may thus be taught the important lesson of the *value of money*. Far too few contemporary young people know the true value of money as they should. This fact accounts in part for the frightful troubles in so many young homes, where there is never enough money to meet all the bills, and the young parents are under constant pressure. In fact, wrangling over money is one of the chief reasons for divorce, according to statistics. Children need to be taught early in life the value of money.

There are four lessons on the value of money every child needs to be taught: 1. how to *make* money; 2. how to *save* money; 3. how to *give* money; and 4. how to *spend* money. Each person should know to make money honestly and properly; how to save it correctly and without becoming a miser; how to give it successfully and wisely to the proper causes for God and humanity; and how to spend it wisely, sensibly, and how to get the most for every dollar spent. My mother-in-law taught us a valuable lesson in spending. She used to say, "It's not a *bargain*, no matter how *cheap* it is, if you don't *need* it!" Many people have wasted hard-earned money for things they will never really need nor find useful, just because they had an urge to spend. Children need long and hard lessons in not misspending their income.

Children should be taught that the allowance is to be spent for sensible things. Some of it may be spent for candy, sodas, and the like, but some should also be reserved for purchasing school supplies, clothes, and other needful articles. Then, too, a share of it should be saved for future needs. (See Chap. 3 #9, in this book.)

7. *The children's part in certain forms of discipline.* Make rules as a family and then decide what punishment shall be meted out when the rules are broken. Never allow the child to *administer* the punishment. This would be unwise and possibly even dangerous. But the child may sit in on the meeting when the punishment is decided. For example, Bill has stolen something from Tom and has used it or destroyed it in some way that it is not replaceable. Let the family council meet and decide what Bill's punishment shall be. When the decision is finalized and there has been a carrying vote, then the parents, or one of them, will carry out the order of the

council. In this way the children are taught the value of civil law and how it works.

8. *Organization.* Use a bulletin board or wall board of some type for listing important things. List events which all need to remember, and list who does what when. Example: Doing dishes — Monday and Wednesday: Grace; Tuesday and Thursday: Velma; Friday and Saturday: Jane.

All important decisions of the family for the week might be listed there also. Notices of many types may be placed on this bulletin board and in this way each is reminded of all coming events and of his place and chores in the home society.

9. *A family crisis.* Discuss the matter openly with the family as much as is possible. Teach each one that no one is to even whisper this to anyone outside the home. Teach family members to keep family secrets within the family circle; teach them as well that each can help to solve family problems.

If the family is securing a new car, discussion may center on what kind and how it shall be paid for, and even what make or type it will be. All are going to enjoy it — why should they not all have a hand in its selection and in the responsibility for its upkeep after it is purchased.

10. *Taking responsibility.* Give each member of the family as much responsibility as he is able to handle. By doing this you teach children that they must learn to take their fair share of the burdens and responsibilities of life. Parents will know how not to overload young children with responsibility, but they will also find that allowing them to share it with the parents will greatly aid in developing dependable and well-developed personalities.

In this way one may teach them to be good cooks, gardeners, repairmen, house cleaners, and launderesses. They will receive valuable lessons in self discipline and self-reliance which will better fit them for life's work.

11. *Long range plans.* When the family forum meets, plans for the long-range future should be discussed. If the oldest child is about ready for college in another year or two, for instance, this should be discussed. All should take part in planning how to help in this matter. Or, other things which are of long-range importance may be discussed, such as next summer's vacation, or the Thanksgiving trip, or the Christmas holiday trip.

Within the family framework there is room for the most liberal education in all the arts of family life. Keep the dignity and sanctity of the family intact at all times. Always keep before the children the fact that "our family doesn't do these things," referring to anything which is below the social standards of sound Christian living. Instead of berating the neighbors who do, just observe that *our family does not do these things.* Keep this motto constantly before the young children and when they are older it will be so ingrained into them that they will not likely bring shame upon the family by indulging in such things. Good sound training for everything necessary for a happy future life can be done within the successful home. The parents should procure all kinds of books for the children's information on every subject necessary for their future happiness — everything from salvation and a sound knowledge of the Bible to sex and a good knowledge of its place in the happy future marriages of the children, as well as in their growing up years and in courtship.

Make the home the university, the church and the government, with a fine community air, in which the whole scope of life's experiences and the necessary information about them may be learned insofar as possible. Read a good life story of Susanna Wesley, mother of John and Charles Wesley, and you will have a fair pattern for this.

12. *Completion of jobs.* Make each child finish what he starts. This rule may seem insignificant, but it is actually of great importance in child training. Children who are consistently allowed to start things which they never finish may never develop a true sense of responsibility. If they get by with their parents, they will expect to get by in later life.

To illustrate, Roberta was allowed to start various things, then leave them for her mother to finish. She never completed a single garment she started without her mother's doing the final work on it. Robert, the younger brother, was never made to finish his work. The rabbit pen he started remained unfinished until his dad finally tossed it away in the trash.

In later life Roberta came home one day complaining that she could not stick it out any longer with John. "Why, has he been unfaithful to you, or beaten you?" her mother asked in surprise.

"No, mother, he's good to me, but there are just so many things in married life I don't like and don't want to do, I simply want to give it up. I would be happier single again."

The mother's pleas went unheeded. Roberta did here just what she had been allowed to do in younger days — she did not finish the task and the home broke up. Robert found that as a man he could never stick to any job for long at a time. He always found some reason to be changing jobs. Of course he never succeeded in the business world. Later, he too, broke up his marriage because he could not stand the grinds of family life. He had never accustomed himself to enduring anything he did not wish to in childhood. His training paid off in adult life in a predictable manner.

Parents should see that children are taught this important and necessary lesson in life — *they must always finish what they start!*

Here are five simple rules which if applied to family life will usually pay good dividends in child training:

Encourage children to have lots of fun at home. Let them invite their friends in for the evening quite often. Pop corn, serve refreshments, and make an interesting evening for them. Never cramp them in their normal fun and play, even though some of it seems a bit rough. They need to work off extra energy.

Tell them good bed-time stories when small. All small children love bed-time stories as a rule. Select the best from literature, in both religious, biblical, and good moral building stories. You can often get ideas across in this way that you cannot instill as successfully in any other way.

Make up your own stories sometimes, too, in which you inculcate deeply religious principles and ideas. You can teach much in this way.

Plan special places to go as often as possible. Children need a variety of interests. You had much better take some time out of a busy life and be with them now than to follow them to court and even perhaps, prison, later in life, because you had no time for them during their formative years.

There is a well-worn story of a famous jurist whose son used to come into his office and ask his dad to take a little time with him. The father was busy working on a great, monumental work of jurisprudence. The great book was one day completed and made its author famous. But the son was also one day completed, so far as his father's influence was concerned. The father was disgraced and humiliated to meet him in jail. "Son, why on earth have you brought this disgrace upon us?"

"Dad, when I needed you as a boy, you never had time for me. You always said, 'Go away, son, I'm busy on my book,' when I asked for your help or for some of your time. You need not come weeping over me now — it's too late. You had your chance to help me but you would not take it, so now go on and enjoy the reputation of your book." He had written a great book, but he had also wrecked a son in the process. Parents need to learn where the *priorities of life lie,* and give their children the time they need.

Make much of birthdays and special occasions. Christian children and young people do not cost parents the tremendous sums that non-Christians often do for many material possessions. Christian parents ought to lay aside extra money for birthday parties and for special occasions, to make these times extra nice for the children and youth.

These occasions also tend to knit family ties and make the children conscious of social, moral and spiritual values connected with them in many instances. If parents tried harder to make the home a more wholesome place for their children, in many instances they might be more successful in saving them for the cause of Christ.

Take the children to church regularly. Religious experience and instruction are essential to the normal development of each child. It is not enough to *send* the children to church — parents need to *accompany* them to God's house for worship and instruction.

No child can develop a properly oriented personality toward life's problems and how to find their solutions without religious guidance. The Sunday school and church provide this guidance in a most excellent manner.

Sometime ago a New York City juvenile judge reported that in over one thousand cases of juvenile offenses brought before him, he had never had a serious case of a young person who was a regular attendant of the Sunday school and church. He reported that there had been two cases of young people who were Sunday school attendants, but upon investigation, it was discovered that one of the fellows did not attend regularly both Sunday school and church, and the other attended Sunday school only intermittently, and did not attend church worship services.

Religion pays large dividends for those who attend to and enjoy its realities. Children need much spiritual nurture and culture in today's world. [6]

Following is an item which will be of interest to parents:

A PARENT'S PRAYER

Help me to the stature of good parenthood.

I pray I may let my child live his own life and not the one I wish I had lived. Therefore, guard me against burdening him with doing what I failed to do, and when tempted to seek this balm for old wounds, strengthen me against my self justification.

[6] Henry A. Bowman, *Marriage for Moderns,* chaps. 10 - 12, pp. 299 - 396.

Help me to see today's missteps in perspective against the long road he must go, and grant me the grace of patience with his slow pace, lest in my impatience I force him into rebellion, retreat, or anxiety.

Give me the precious wisdom of knowing when to smile at the small mischiefs of his age and when to give him the haven of firmness against the impulses which in his heart he fears and cannot master.

In time of needed punishment give me a warm heart and a gentle voice so he may feel the rule of order is his friend and clasp it to his soul to be his conscience. Help me to let him know in advance what the consequences of his misdeeds will be. Help me to hear the anguish in his heart through the din of angry words or across the gulf of brooding silence, and having heard, give me the grace to bridge the gap between us with understanding warmth before speaking my own quick retorts, and stay my tongue also from the words which would chill his confiding in me.

Still from my voice and smooth from my brow all that mars infectious serenity and joy in living; rather let my face so shine that these later years will seem to him a promised land toward which to strive.

I pray that I may raise my voice more in joy at what he is than in vexation at what he has done; so each day he may grow in sureness of himself.

Help me to hold him with such warmth as will give him friendliness toward fellow man; then give me the fortitude to free him to go strongly on his way.

Then as I see him striding forward eagerly, self-sure, friendly, and in good conscience, my grateful heart will swell with joy.

— Dr. Marion B. Durfee
Medical Director,
Pasadena Child Guidance Clinic

Chapter 6

Sane Sex Sense

Outside of religious experience, there are no more sacred or ennobling experiences than those associated with sex in its true and proper functions. Sex is the gateway to life, and the experiences in connection with its proper functions are of the highest order. Love, in its basically biological and psychological sense, is a most thrilling and enlivening experience. The basic urge for survival, or for reproduction, out of which the sex urge arises, is as near to the fountain of life as one can come. And yet, how tragic that this most beautiful of all human experiences should become so sordid and vile as it has become because of our misunderstanding of its true nature and the general misuse of it.

One of the major problems of most parents is the matter of properly educating their children about the important functions of sex in life. Most young people, especially girls, who come for counseling report that their parents have not told them anything about sex, or that what they were told was inadequate.

When such uninformed children become young people, still lacking proper knowledge about sex and its relation to life, many bitter experiences result. The cost in anxiety and embarrassment is great. Not only have many premarriage pregnancies resulted from this lack of information, but much sorrow after marriage often results from it as well. A young married lady who came for counseling stated that she was not free to discuss sex matters with her mother. She explained, "I cannot talk with my mother even today about such matters. I guess it is what she did to me as a child. She never told me anything about sex. When menstruation began I was away from home. It frightened me almost to death." Another young married woman reported a similar circumstance. "Mother never told me anything about sex. I learned about menstruation by accident from some neighbors. When I was fifteen, I thought if a boy kissed you you would get pregnant!"

Another young woman reported that when she was nineteen she had her first serious courtship. The first time her boyfriend kissed her she became nervous and felt a tingling awakening inside her — a normal sexual response to the kiss. Of this experience she said, "I thought I was *getting pregnant!*"

Boys are often just as ill-informed. Recently, a young man reported that he had deep difficulties in his teen years because he had no idea what a girl's body looked like. The curiosity disturbed him. Some boys are doubtless driven to "experiment" with girls sexually just because of this ignorance and the need to satisfy curiosity. Hundreds of young men have all but wrecked their marriages at the start because of their total ignorance about sex matters and the proper approach to married life.

It is the duty of the parents to teach children and young people all the needed factors about sex and life. If instruction is given properly, untold sorrow and wreckage of life can be avoided in most instances.

In counseling with parents who want to tell their children about sex, I have noticed most of them complain that they do not know *how to tell* their children properly. Likely, most parents themselves have had inadequate information about these matters as children and teen-agers, so they feel unprepared to tell their own children. For this reason it seems wise to give a few important pointers on how to give this information to children.

1. *Tell them only what they ask for at one time.* Perhaps the following story will illustrate the folly of some well-intentioned parents, who, when trying to tell children the story of sex, tell too much. Martin Simon told the story of a fellow who took his sick horse to the veterinarian for treatment. The first dose of medicine did the horse so much good that the fellow decided to give him the whole bottle the next night, so as to cure him much more quickly. The next morning when the man went to the stable he found the horse dead! Information given by the parent should be given in small enough doses not to damage the child. [1]

Probably the best rule is to tell the child merely what he asks for at each time, without much elaboration. When he wants to know more he will likely be back requesting more information. To tell a child more than is necessary to satisfy his passing curiosity is like over-stuffing him with food — it does no good and may do harm. He is probably not prepared to accept it all; therefore, it will tend to trouble his mind because he does not fully understand.

[1] Martin P. Simon, *Points for Parents,* p. 13.

As to the age for imparting this information and the way in which it may best be done, one authority gives this advice:

> Any time after your child is two and one half to three . . . you may expect the question, "Where do babies come from?" . . . Answer simply and matter of factly, "They grow inside their mothers." This will in most cases suffice for sometime. Then they will ask some other question, one which usually elicits the information that the baby was once a tiny egg, which grew until the baby was ready to live in the world. . . . When your children ask you where they came from and other questions, they are entitled to honest answers. You are on the spot. How you help them at this age is a measure of your success as a parent. . . . You must know the facts — and not guess — and state them clearly. Give the essentials; don't overload with details. . . . He'll probably ask about pregnancy, birth, fertilization and mating, and usually in that order. . . . In answering, be friendly, not evasive, not vague, certainly not jocular or frivolous. Be serious, but not sentimental. Never conclude with, "That is why we love you so!" And *never, never,* say, "That is the reason why you should love mother and daddy. [2]

The child need not be bothered at this juncture with sentimental lectures on loving his parents. This mixes the business of birth and life with the ideas of love and affection. He should not merely love his parents because they are his parents, but for the value and worth he attaches to them as human beings. Let him learn to love out of the depths of appreciation, not by the matter of dependency.

Soon the youngster will begin to wonder what part the daddy plays in all this business of being born. Here is generally the most difficult thing for the mother or father to explain to him, but sooner or later, it must be explained.

Children at this period pop all sorts of interesting questions. When you explain to Janet, for instance, that the baby "grows in mommie's stomach till it's large enough to live outside," her next question will likely be a clincher: "Does daddy grow babies in his stomach?" When you answer that he does not, she may then wish to know, "Then what makes him to be a daddy?" Now, you are stuck with a most difficult question. The father role is far harder to explain than the mother role. Yet, you must be fair and unafraid, answering without trying to evade the issue. Otherwise, you create the feeling in the child that something is not exactly *right* about the father's part. And this could be damaging to him. So, you must be ready with some answer. Maybe if you simply explain here that the

[2] Jean C. Phillips, *Better Homes and Gardens Baby Book,* p. 187.

father plants the seed in the mother from which the baby grows you will be able to satisfy the need for the moment. But more explanation will soon be needed.

Perhaps you could explain that the father places the seed in the mother when they make love together sometimes. Later, when the child is old enough to realize more fully the function of the father in the birth of a child, it can be explained more fully.

In a recent lecture series on counseling parents at the Narramore Christian Counseling Center, Rosemead, California, it was stated that out of one thousand young people who had had proper home training about sex, only *one* of them became a sex offender. In another survey, it was discovered that out of one thousand sex offenders, hardly *any* of them had had proper sex education. Can you see the tremendous importance in proper sex education? There is no better place for it than the home.

2. *Keep sex knowledge on a high level.* This is essential for youth. Sex is simply a part of life — and a dear and important part. We should cease forever to treat it as if it were some deep, dark secret, or a hidden mystery, shrouded in all sorts of shame. No, sex is beautiful, pure, clean and good. It only becomes evil when it is misused. We should teach our children the nobility, sublimity and utter beauty of sex life. Sex affects the *whole person,* in every way. It is what makes the difference between boys and girls, men and women. It is related to the total life pattern and not just to the bodily organs with which it must be associated. We should think of these organs just as we do our hands, feet, nose, eyes, and ears. They are just as pure as all other parts of the body. We should always think of them in this light. Associate love and sex life with beautiful mountains, lovely scenic beauties, huge waterfalls, beautiful flowers and good, inspiring music. In this way, you can help your child to make the proper associations about sex life.

Whenever sex is associated with evil things, it invariably fixes deeply in the child's mind a bad approach toward normal sex life. One should never refer to it in any way that causes the child to think of it as evil or unwholesome. Feelings of guilt can be created in the child's mind which may never be fully erased in an entire lifetime, despite later education to the contrary. Ideas once implanted in childhood, especially between the ages of two and seven, are definitely *fixed* and are often almost impossible to totally erase.

3. *Parents need to prepare themselves for sex education in the home.* In order for parents to know how to tell their children about sex properly they need to be properly informed themselves. In this volume there is hardly room for all that needs to be said on this

subject. The following books are recommended for preparing parents for this sacred duty: Dr. Clyde M. Narramore's book, *How to Tell Your Children About Sex* may be obtained either from the publisher, Zondervan Publishing House, 1415 Lake Drive, Grand Rapids, Michigan, 49506, or from the Narramore Christian Foundation, 1409 N. Walnut Grove Avenue, Rosemead, California, 91770. The price is $1.00.

One may also go to the public library and secure books on this subject. Ask the librarian for books which show illustrations of the various organs of the body and their functions. If you explain that you want books to better inform yourself as how to tell your children about sex, the librarian will be able to help you much more successfully. There is nothing to be embarrassed about in asking for such books.

William C. Hendricks' booklet, *God's Temples,* is most helpful. It may be ordered from the publisher, Wm. B. Eerdmans, Grand Rapids, Michigan.

4. *Encourage your teen-agers to share their problems with you.* Every counselor finds that young people as a whole relate to him that it is difficult to discuss the matter of sex with his parents. There has been far too much "hush-hush" about sex in the home. Consequently, young people either think their parents are unprepared to discuss the subject with them, or that they are ashamed to do so; hence, the young people tend to go on either uninformed or to seek information in unworthy places. Either of these roads can lead to ruin.

5. *Accept sex as a normal part of life.* This is exactly what children will always do unless they are inhibited otherwise by teachings or the strange actions and silences of the parents about sex matters. If the children are allowed to think of sex as a wholesome part of the self life and to respect it as such, they will not likely develop the evil-minded view that develops from wrong emphasis upon it and improper information about its functions. The "hush-hush" attitude of parents — the fact that sex is never mentioned — or the fact that pregnant mothers among the family's friends are referred to in whispered tones, as if something were wrong, may instill in the minds of children all sorts of bad ideas about sex. It is only natural for them to jump to the conclusion that anything so secretive must be wrong, when nothing could be farther from the truth. Sex is beautiful in its proper place and should always be idealized by parents and held up to children as a grand and wonderful function of life. It is not to be tampered nor played with, nor to be exploited by vain experimentation by youth. It is sacred and

has God's stamp of approval as an experience for married people only.

One of the finest discussions coming to my attention of late with reference to the sex problems of parents and children in the training period is found in English and Pearson's book, *Emotional Problems of Living.*[3] This book may be found in the public library. Some of the latest information existent about sex knowledge, training the child properly, sex-play and its relation to normal life, will be found in this volume.

NOTE: An exceptionally good book which every parent should read on the subject of homosexuality is *Growing Up Straight, or What Every Parent Should Know About Homosexuality,* by Peter and Barbara Wyden, M.D. It will be very enlightening and helpful in guiding the child through the early years when dangers of this evil are sometimes strongest.

Chapter 7

Troublesome Teens

The Apostle Paul exhorted, "Children, obey your parents in the Lord: for this is right. Honor thy father and mother; (which is the first commandment with promise;) That it may be well with thee, and thou mayest live long on the earth" (Eph. 6:1-3). "Children" here is a generic term and does not refer merely to small children, but to all young people. Even after one is married and away from home, he has no right to dishonor his parents in any way. Often parental advice and counsel, if wisely taken, may prevent sorrows in the homes of children married and rearing their own families.

As if in the same breath he needed to say a word to parents, Paul exhorted, "And ye fathers, provoke not your children to wrath; but bring them up in the nurture and admonition of the Lord" (Eph. 6:4). This is also a most excellent and needful passage for parents. Far too many parents provoke their children to wrath by unnecessary means and then wonder why their children do not ad-

[3] O. S. English and G. J. Pearson, *Emotional Problems of Living,* pp. 99-111.

mire and love them any more than they do. Where true love between parents and children is lasting, there must be cooperative
living.

There are several problems which parents and teen-agers must
face in home life. We have selected what we feel are the most outstanding ones for discussion here. It is hoped that teen-agers will
read this section of the book with as eager interest as their parents.

1. *Understanding and properly guiding teen-agers* is a major
problem for parents. Possibly one of the most difficult problems of
the teens is here. Blessed indeed are the parents who understand
their youngsters. There are several reasons why parents generally
do not fully understand teen-agers:

2. *The "gap" is great between the teen years of parents and children.* This problem points up a significant change in the cultural
patterns of our lives. Most parents who are between thirty-five and
forty-five were reared in a different culture-pattern from that which
envelops contemporary teen-agers. Often parents are so busy making
a living and participating in the interests of their own age groups
that they do not find time to breathe the atmosphere of their teen-
agers; for this failure they pay the heavy price of not understanding
just what makes their own teen-agers "tick." If they took more time
to try to understand their language, mannerisms, moral slants and
even their religious views, they would much more easily understand
what is guiding teens. They would also understand teen *problems*
much better and be more able to help their youngsters with them.

A large majority of teen-age boys and girls who come to me for
counseling complain about two things most bitterly: (a) "My parents don't understand me. They never seem to realize that we live
in two different worlds." (b) "My parents never told me anything
about sex, and these important things about life."

These two complaints are registered by a majority of all young
people who go to counselors or pastors for help. We can generally
discount a considerable part of the first one on the basis of parent-
child hostility; this emotion is perfectly natural, even with deeply
religious young people. But we cannot ignore the second complaint. It lies deeply embedded in the genuine lack of parents to
get information and help their youngsters in a needful area. One
of the major purposes of this book is to help parents to bridge this
"gap" and to give their children the necessary information, assur-
ances, help and guidance they need. There is no better way to
crucify your son, or especially your daughter — than upon a cross
of wilful neglect, neglect to lovingly give the proper information
about these mighty streams of sex life. God made you responsible

as parents to teach your children. If you fail them here, you have failed them miserably and possibly for all time to come!

3. *Parents have largely forgotten what it was like to be a teen-ager.* Either their teens were unhappy and they have subconsciously repressed their memories, or, fortunately, they were very happy and never discovered the rougher side of teen life. In any case, many parents have dull memories of teen years when it comes to understanding their own offspring. They often look at teens in amazement and say something like this: "If I had acted like that when I was a teen-ager, my parents would have beaten the tar out of me!" Or, "I just can't understand *why* you have to be this way"; or, "Why do you want to do such things?" or, "I never did such things as a teen-ager!" Immediately, the teen-ager knows he is not understood, nor are his position, thinking and wishes appreciated by his parents. He then feels at a loss to know what to do or where to turn. Sometimes there is a friendly parent in the neighborhood who happens to understand teen-agers, to whom he will turn in frustration for help. If this person is a safe guide, his help is beneficial; but should he prove to have an unwholesome influence, the teen-ager can be headed for serious problems.

4. *Communication between parents and teen-agers often breaks down.* Here is one of the most serious problems. Often parents and teen-agers continue to talk after all true communication has broken down. *Communication* is far more than merely *talking*. It is getting each other's *ideas* and *feelings* across and having them *accepted* and *understood*. A parent does not have to *approve* of a teen-ager's ideas or moods to accept and understand them. But teen-agers know pretty well the moment their ideas, moods, or feelings are rejected by their parents.

To illustrate; Jane was arguing with her mother about the dress she wanted for the high school senior banquet. Her mother did not agree at all with her as to the style of the dress nor the price Jane wanted to pay for it. "But, Mother, it's not the style nor the price that bothers me so much as the fact that *you don't seem to understand* what all this means to me. You act and talk as if I had no *feelings* at all and could just go and sit there and represent you and what you want and be perfectly happy. Oh, Mother, you are *impossible* at times — you simply don't get my *feelings* at all!"

Similar situations often arise with boys. Fathers often provoke their sons to anger by their thoughtlessness and determined self-will. If they would only sit down and explain things to them, there would be little or no problem. But a stern command, without any explanation or the desire to even discuss the matter on the parent's part, often drives the son to rebellion.

Often by their poor judgment, misunderstanding and lack of being able to enter into the moods and feelings of their youngsters, parents encourage and help to generate enough rebellion in their youngsters to destroy any religious feelings they have ever had. Then the parents simply cannot understand why the children do not want to accept and take up the way of the Cross. If parents spent a bit more time trying to understand their youngsters instead of treating them as mere children, they could go much farther in leading them to Christ.

If and when parents can bridge these three major gaps, they are well on the way to being understanding and helpful parents. If they cannot or for some reason do not care to try to bridge them, they will most likely lose their teen-agers. If the children ever become stalwart Christians, or even good wholesome citizens, some hand other than theirs will have provided the miraculous touch. Someone with a warm heart, deep sympathy, and understanding for the teen-ager and his needs may be nearby to effect a rescue. If not, there is a high ratio of possibility that the teen-ager will drift away into an undesirable life so far as the Christian way is concerned. It is pitiful to see parents daily "crucifying" their children upon crosses of neglect, ignorance and self-will. Millions are doing so.

One should not infer that parents in general are not interested in their children; they are. But they need to be interested deeply enough to go these "second miles" in outlay of self, time, and energy to understand and be cooperative with the teen-agers as they should. Some parents tend to be too much lord and master of their castle. If children do not wish to bow and come under, that is just too bad for *them*. Unfortunately, it is also *just too bad for parents.*

The explanation of a hippie in Hollywood, California, will illustrate this point. He stated that he had become a hippie because his parents would not allow him to do certain things in his home which he felt as a teen-ager he wanted to do. They simply told him if he wished to wear his long hair, dress carelessly and parade the streets with others in like manner, he would *have to get out!* So he did. He was making good money selling hippie papers and said he intended to make a career of the armed services when he got some of this youthful bubbling out of his system. He might have been saved to the cause of the home had the parents had more parental love, sympathy and understanding.

5. *Teen-years are a common and serious problem.* Just what makes a teen-ager rebellious? There is no blanket answer to this question,

for there may be as many reasons as there are homes and teen-agers. Two teen-agers in the same home may be rebellious against their parents, or home rules for entirely *different* reasons! Some of these reasons follow:

(a) *There may be lack of complete understanding on the part of both parents and young people, as seen above.* Out of this lack the younger one may feel there is no other way out but some form of rebellion. Rebellion may take several forms: pouting, refusing to obey parents, talking back when this can be done successfully, running away from home, doing things contrary to the known wishes of parents, becoming irritable and uncooperative. Sometimes it may also manifest itself in some form of emotional or even bodily sickness. There is the case of the girl who wanted to marry a young man to whom the father objected. Outwardly obedient to his refusal to give his consent, the girl developed a serious case of arthritis. Upon examination, the doctor found out about the emotional tension between the daughter and her father. He recommended that the father relent and allow her to marry. He did so and the girl was well in a few weeks. But again the father renewed his opposition, and again the girl became almost paralyzed with arthritis. Finally, he gave consent and she regained complete health. Here, rebellion found its way out through bodily illness.

The author remembers a case of a teen-ager in rebellion who developed a partial paralysis of one side of her face and one side of the body. After several days of hospitalization and every known test, doctors could not find any cause for the paralysis nor any damage to the brain. I visited, counseled, and had prayer with her, having known her from childhood. In a reasonable while the paralysis slowly disappeared and she returned to normal life. But with her return to health, the rebellion had also greatly subsided. Shortly afterward she became a Christian.

Sometimes, too, mild forms of mental illnesses may occur as the outlet for pent-up rebellion. This occurrence is usually much less frequent than other outlets which rebellion takes.

(b) *Rebellion may also grow out of deep psychological needs for the young person to develop more personal dependability.* Nature has given us parents to help us through the early and necessary period of development. But sometimes parents hang on and become over-protective and create psychological and sociological problems with which the teen-ager finds difficulty in coping. Then rebellion may be the only way the young person sees out of his dilemma. English and Pearson, after discussing the need for emancipation from parental protectiveness and its problems, say:

Certain factors that are inimical to maturation exist in the adolescent and in the parent. The adolescent has (a) the continuing emotional need to be cared for, (b) the reluctance to accept responsibility, (c) the fear of criticism when responsibility is taken, and (d) the lack of desire to serve and cooperate with adults. In the parent, on the other hand, there exists — and it is usually unconscious — (a) the desire to retain dominance or control over the youngster, (b) the difficulty of sharing his love and loyalty with others, (c) the fear that he will come to harm in the outside world, and (d) an underestimation of the adolescent's strength to function independently.[1]

These conflicts often make the necessary emancipation for the younger person in the home an almost insurmountable mountain for some parents and teen-agers. Parental *dominance* can become a serious hazard, especially if the young person happens to have certain personality weaknesses and develops an unnatural amount of dependence upon the parents. Two Christian parents brought a lovely daughter well in her thirties to me for counseling. She was near nervous exhaustion and on the verge of collapse. Consultation revealed that when the mother had had serious surgery and the daughter feared she would be bereft of her, she virtually collapsed. After the mother's recovery, the girl slowly improved somewhat. The counseling session revealed that the mother was over-dominant and the daughter over-dependent. She was nervous, rigid, fidgety, and restless, and the mother did almost all the talking for the girl. After the parents left the counseling room and we spent a little time together, the daughter became calm and discussed her whole problem sensibly and quietly. Her nervousness almost entirely disappeared. She had almost been ruined by the over-dominance of a gracious and saintly mother. Her greatest need was complete emancipation from her parents.

Another way girls sometimes displace rebellion against parents is by *becoming pregnant* before marriage. This statement may appear strange to some, but statistics show that almost fifty percent of pre-marital pregnancies are traceable to some form of rebellion against the parents by the girl. Sometimes it takes the form of a means to gain marriage permission when it has been refused; sometimes it is done for pure "spite," the girl not stopping to think that she is really hurting herself most of all. Sometimes, too, the girl is not totally conscious that her rebellion brings about this act. At any rate, mothers and daughters will do well to talk this situation over and let the light of reason, cold common sense, and good hard future think-

[1] O. S. English and G. J. Pearson, *Emotional Problems of Living*, p. 376.

ing play their part in helping the young girl see the senselessness of such a venture.

Ignorance about sex, too, contributes a great deal to premarital pregnancies. Sometimes the girl may even be unconsciously fighting back at her mother for allowing her to be so ignorant at her age. Mothers will do well to inform their girls about sex in every way well before they are in their mid-teens. The young girl needs complete information about the male's part in sexual experience, too. Otherwise, she may be tempted out of curiosity to experiment. Girls should be told that complete intercourse is *not necessary* for them to get pregnant! If semen is spilled near the vaginal entrance, sufficient sperm may get into the vaginal tract to cause fertilization. Many young people hold to the notion that so long as the penis is not fully inserted into the vaginal tract, the girl is still a virgin and no harm can come to her. Whatever the moral idea may be, the biological one is most certainly risky and should never be allowed to occur.

(c) *Rebellion may sometimes grow out of over-harshness on the part of parents.* Fathers and mothers are not to "provoke" their children to wrath by unnecessary harshness. Young people in the home wish to be trusted as adults when they feel they have achieved that status. Often a teen-ager will come around much better if he is treated as if he were a person, rather than merely ordered around as if he were an irresponsible child. True, sometimes young people do *act childish*, but all the tests made of their ability to respond to life's situations prove quite conclusively that most late teen-agers are quite well equipped to become adult in their outlook, and often in their decisions and actions. In this light, parents should give them every consideration possible.

To make a teen-ager completely responsible for the outcome of his decisions and actions will often make him more cautious than if a parent tells him what to do and accepts the responsibility for him. Nothing brings a person to maturation quite so fast as responsibility for his own decisions and actions. Parents need to help teen-agers make the better choices, where they can; but by and large, teen-agers also need to be encouraged to make decisions for which they will take the consequences. Sometimes parents feel they just cannot leave such important matters to John and Betty when they are so young. But it is wise to do so, then watch how they turn out. If they are encouraged in decision making for small matters, they will be better equipped when they have to tackle some of the really big ones, such as choosing a mate for life, or their life's work.

Young people must learn that rebellion, for whatever reason, does not pay off in the gold of happiness and successful adjustment to life. It may be fun momentarily to "stump" Mom and Dad and watch them sweat it out, but it will not be a worthy memory when the adult years have come to fruition. Better grit your teeth, hold your tongue and say "O.K., I'll have my own sweet way some day!" and let it go at that.

You will be much happier that you did when the golden years of full-blown adulthood are upon you and your own children are about you. After all, young friend, teen years are mostly something to be "endured" anyhow — unless you are adjusted to them so that you can really "enjoy them." Most people agree with Walter Pitkin, who wrote *Life Begins at Forty*, when he cried, "Not for all the world would I be a teen-ager again!" However, if you adjust properly to the teen years and remember they are mostly "harness years" — that is, *training years* — you can have a great deal of fun and come through them with no bad memories. Whatever your lot, remember, "Obedience is better than sacrifice." An ancient king found this out at an awful price! You can find it out much less expensively and more profitably, too.

6. *Social problems play a heavy role in the teen years.* Parents and teen-agers must face these together. A cooperative spirit will make these problems less difficult and far more easily solved. There are problems here and no one can avoid them, for they are simply a part of the nature and manner of growing up and becoming adjusted to life, and there is no dodging them. Only *retarded* children have no social problems. Even the most obedient and deeply devout Christian teen-agers develop social problems of one kind or another.

The ultimate goal for a Christian home is the successful solution of such problems. Let us face a few of these problems and determine that together we will whip them:

(a) *Don't shove children or young people together.* Parents sometimes make the mistake of thinking it is "cute" to see boys and girls paired off in the sub-teen and early teen years. They encourage a certain amount of pre-courtship pairing of this kind. Mothers are often *far too anxious* to get their daughters started right in courtship. Possibly there is a subconscious fear that they will not find a mate and be unfortunate maiden ladies.

In the first place, most maiden ladies are *not unfortunate*. It is a thousand times *better* to be single and desire marriage than to be married and *regretting it,* as untold thousands are today! There are many *frigid women* for whom marriage is a horrible chore, who would have been far happier in the single state. They have no need nor desire for sex and no desire for children. Both are an endless grind upon them and they make their husbands miserable as well. One of the disadvantages of our Western culture is that marriage has somehow become a "status symbol," far out of all proportion to its necessity for genuine happiness and usefulness. The same Paul who said, "I will therefore that the younger women marry, bear children, guide the house . . ." (I Tim. 5:14), also said, "I say therefore to the unmarried and widows, It is good for them if they abide even as I . . ." (I Cor. 7:8). Marriage is the golden ideal of every girl largely because it has been cultivated into her as the only proper state for an adult woman. But this is not true at all. There is no scriptural law which leads one to believe that marriage is necessary or even desirable for all women.

Think for a moment of all the everlasting good that has come to the world because of the unselfishly dedicated lives of multitudes of single women, or others who devoted their lives after widowhood to some great cause. What would the world have done without Florence Nightingale, mother of modern nursing and her myriads of dedicated followers in this profession? Or Evangeline Booth, who turned down a hundred proposals for marriage from commoners and the wealthy to lead the Salvation Army to greater triumphs of Christian service? Or Frances E. Willard, who gave her life for the cause of temperance? A multitude of dedicated missionary ladies, school teachers and countless others could be added to this list, but these will illustrate what has been said. Marriage is not at all necessary for every girl in order that she may achieve complete satisfaction and lasting happiness in life, as well as offer to the world some of its best service.

Pushing boy-girl parties too soon can be the beginning of ultimately serious problems, both emotionally, socially and perhaps, morally. Allow the natural instincts to initiate boy-girl relations at the proper time and you will have enough problems without encouraging them prematurely.

(b) *Allow young people to develop as normally as possible.* Do not cramp them, too soon, into molds for which they are not yet ready. Sometimes by trying to put them on adult behavior patterns we only drive them into forms of rebellion. It is most embarrassing to a young person before his peers to be cramped into an unnatural situation.

Church people often expect too advanced behavior from young Christians and thereby cripple some of them. Sometimes zealous persons tend to push young people into Christian service far too early. Many a young man who may have become a successful

minister later on was pushed forward too fast and "ruined" before
his day really dawned. Paul warned Timothy to "Lay hands suddenly on no man . . ." (I Tim. 5:22). He meant do not shove
young men forward before holy orders too soon. Let them mature
a little. If a younger person feels the call to the ministry and wants
to be so recognized and given openings for service, this is fine.
But one should not be pressed into service ahead of his feeling that
he ought to be in such service. Again, Paul warned of too early
ordination: "Not a novice, lest he be puffed up with pride and fall
into the condemnation of the devil" (I Tim. 3:6).

Sometimes church people have demanded adult behavior of young
people by trying to put "forty-year-old heads on fifteen-year-old
shoulders." They have never succeeded. In consequence of this
attitude by adults, we have in our churches *a lot of heads sitting
around with no shoulders to put them on!* We have driven the
youth away by over-pressing them.

(c) *There is the problem of a too restricted friendship.* Girls
tend to this problem more than boys. Boys gravitate toward the
"gang" spirit in groups. Often girls will choose one close girl friend
and become intertwined with her to the detriment of them both,
thus narrowing opportunity for personality development, possibly
warping the personality, and hindering proper personality growth.
Unless there is the sunshine of many different personalities inter-
acting upon the young person's life, his own personality may not
grow and blossom as it should and could under the right circumstances.

It is never a good policy to have only one special friend. Better
to have a special friend but also many others with whom one is free
to visit and do things at any time. Sometimes such girl friends become jealous of each other and create unnecessary problems. And
once in a while, in certain instances, a case of homosexuality may
develop if two girls are allowed to be too much alone, especially
if they sleep together and spend a great deal of time in each other's
homes. Girls who tend to be "loners" get along better with fewer
friends. But this is just the opposite of what they really *need.* They
need to spread out their friendships, get acquainted with far more
people and see what the world of people is really like. By widened
acquaintance and knowledge they may overcome this seclusive ten-
dency which, normally, is not a healthy outlook on life. The same
applies to boys who occasionally manifest recluse moods and with-
drawing patterns. Parents should see that little two-person cliques
do not go too far, for young people can be definitely harmed emotionally by such behavior. To have one special friend is of course

not harmful to anyone, but to keep oneself aloof from all other young people is dangerous and detrimental to the young person who needs to develop a wider interest in people and in life.

7. *Going steady too young is another teen-age problem.* This problem must be squarely faced and properly solved by teen-agers and their parents, if the teen-ager is not to be greatly impaired or possibly ruined for life.

Going steady too early may not only be a problem, but it may also be a symptom of another problem or problems lying even deeper, such as an unhappy home, over-dominant parents, fear and insecurity on the part of the young person, or over-sexual stimulation, causing the young person to be seeking early marriage as a way out of what he feels is a bad situation. In any of these or similar cases the young person needs counseling to help him to face his real problem and deal with it. Marriage is not the answer to any of the above problems and cannot help to solve them, except in a temporary way. One who feels the strong need to go steady needs to have special help and attention to help him or her solve the even more profound problem. This should be done before it becomes a *fixed factor* in life which may only give difficulty all one's life.

Many times lack of proper training about all the above matters drives the young person onward on a course which is neither wise nor good. Often, too, the young person does not know where to turn for the much-needed help. Seek help from your pastor or from a professional counselor. Narramore Christian Foundation, 1409 North Walnut Grove Avenue, Rosemead, California, offers excellent Christian counselors ready to help anyone who may come or write for help. Also, the author welcomes such cases and often does considerable counseling by mail at Christian Counseling Service, 11326 Ranchito St., El Monte, California. If there seems to be no one else to help you, please contact someone by mail. To do so will pay rich dividends.

Now let us look at the young peoples' side of the argument in favor of going steady at a young age, say between thirteen and seventeen. They can offer in its defense at least the following points: It gives one self-confidence to know someone cares that much about him or her; offers a steady date when one needs a social companion at formal affairs; keeps one from boredom — there's always someone to turn to; offers someone to share life's experiences with; and it enriches young life with deep emotional experiences much earlier than usual.

One may add the fact that the young person develops the *feeling* of appreciation for the opposite sex by coming to know someone else better. The girl, especially, has a sense of security, since she always has a date for social occasions. It may be argued, too, that going steady early makes for better understanding of boy-girl relationships, and perhaps offers a possibility of marriage sooner in life than if one did not go steady early.

On the surface these reasons all sound like possibly good defenses for the fad. But on the other hand, there are few of all these aspects which may not be had by the active, alert and careful person without going steady. They can generally be found in boy-girl relationships outside and apart from going steady. Young people cannot afford, for only a few months of fleeting pleasure which will never be missed as adults, to run the risk of ruining a whole life. Here are some reasons why going steady too young is not good.

(a) *It may warp the personalities of the young people involved.* For instance, if Kate and Tom date steadily from ages fourteen to seventeen, they get to know almost no one else besides themselves. They miss the mainstream of a host of other fine young people they desperately *need to know* in helping them develop normally adjusted healthy personalities. Soon this period of life is gone forever, and they have forever lost some of the most valuable experiences to be had.

Such steady couples tend to spend too much time with each other, alone. Sometimes they become withdrawn and develop depressive moods which may later result in bad mental or emotional health. Often times, most fortunately, such romances break up when the young people involved mature a bit more, but then both are left more or less "stranded" because they know almost no other young people intimately.

(b) *Often the girl is exposed to the possibility of a pre-marital pregnancy.* The possibility is far greater than if she did not go steady. This in itself is both a serious and entirely unnecessary risk to run.

(c) *Sometimes a young person gets "stuck" with an emotionally disturbed person who begs pitifully not to be ditched.* Such a disturbed person needs professional help. You cannot give it to him, and you are only running the risk of hurting him and making him even more emotionally unbalanced. Break with him soon and let him get the help he needs.

Art Linkletter and Dear Abby once discussed this problem of going steady too early on one of Art's broadcasts. After Abby had stated why it was not good for young teen-agers to go steady, Art added his comment: "I think going steady for thirteen to sixteen-year-olds is for the *birds!*" Psychologists, sociologists and professional counselors would fully agree with him.

(d) *Going steady too young may not only warp the personality, endanger too early marriages, throw the girl in danger of premarital pregnancy, but it may also hinder one in finding the proper mate.* It may rob one of a lifetime of happiness and success that can never come to him — just because a person refuses to recognize the danger signals. It can, and often does, bring bitterness and sorrow and tragedy beyond any words one can speak or write.

A sixteen-year-old girl can hardly hope to marry anyone who is properly prepared for life, unless as a rarity, she may happen to marry a man ten years her senior who is prepared for his work and will become an outstanding man. A few marriages out of the dim past may shine forth. Marriages today, however, are different from those of the past; they need much more adhesive power to hold them together than marriages did a century ago.

One psychologist has quite correctly remarked that "marriage is an institution for adults, and children have no business in it." Parents should try from the time children are small to implant in their minds the ideal that marriage should not take place until young people are well prepared for it by having finished college, business college, or a career preparation, such as an R.N.'s nursing course, or other preparation. They should be well into their twenties for the most happy and successful marriages to ensue.

(e) *Going steady too young can also become an educational hazard.* Often young "steadies" become so emotionally involved with each other that their studies are neglected. If allowed to do so, "steadies" will hang on the phone with each other for an hour or more at the time in the evening when homework needs attention. Sometimes their grades decline and all sorts of problems arise. Their minds are so affected that they cannot study well for thinking of the involvement and making plans for dates and good times. Sometimes, too, such young people drop out of school unless forced to continue by their parents. They are unable to see at this age the need and advantage of an education. One's whole life may in this way be seriously hindered, or even damaged. Boys sometimes drop out to work so they can have more to give to the beloved one, thereby ruining possibilities for future success in their life's work. Girls quit to marry and often choose husbands of far poorer quality than if they had become properly educated. These factors are far more serious than most young people can realize, as will be seen in the chapter on marriage.

8. *Getting along with teen-agers is an important problem.* It stands to reason that this is also a teen-ager's problem as well as a parental one, and it is hoped that the teen-agers as well as parents will read what is here discussed.

Teen-agers are intelligent people and should be treated as such by parents. Teeners today in high school cover more material than the average college student did thirty or forty years ago. Their huge textbooks are sometimes staggering, and they are required to do much research and to produce intellectually stimulating research papers.

Sometimes parents fail to recognize the needs of teeners in their homes. Marilee Morell did a research paper for an undergraduate course in "Guiding the Adolescent" — referring to teen-agers — in which she discovered that teeners have the following basic needs:

> For exploration and adventure
> For creativity
> For sharing personal experiences with others
> For personal recognition by others
> For learning to live with authority
> For developing a sense of achievement
> For personal commitment to some worthy cause. [2]

If the young person is to be a happy and well-adjusted individual, these needs should be met. His parents should help him meet these needs and make the proper adjustments to life.

Of special interest, too, are the religious *values* held by a majority of American teen-agers. Parents should help their children find and sustain such values. Doing so will greatly aid them in a better working relationship with their teen young people. In a special research project by Remmers and Radler on teen-age religious values in particular, the following results emerged:

> The typical teen-ager today retains a favorable attitude toward the church, attends services about once a week and says prayers once or twice a day. His religious beliefs usually agree with those of his parents. If there is a disagreement between the parents, the adolescent is more likely to agree with his mother's religious values than with those of his father. This makes him more of a churchgoer, since the typical mother of a teen-age child attends at least twice a month, while the father does not usually go to church that often.
>
> The average teen-ager thinks of God not as a person but as an omnipotent and omniscient bodiless spirit who exists everywhere. On the average, the teen believes faith serves better than logic in solving

[2] Marilee Morrell, "Guiding Adolescents," unpublished research paper.

life's important problems. He feels that his prayers are sometimes answered. He believes in the hereafter and expects his place there to be determined by his conduct here on earth. He believes that God guided or inspired the writing of the Bible, and that a good human society could not be built without such supernatural help. [3]

9. *Proper planning by the family so that each one knows what to expect is also important.* It relieves tensions that build up in a family, or helps to keep them from arising in the first place. Too many homes are a sort of helter-skelter place, held together largely by the fact that the family must have somewhere to find good shelter — they are far from being real "homes." Young lives are shaped by the environment of the home; if order prevails they will respect it and abide by the principles taught therein. Myers has shed some light on this point in the following quotation: "A college lad, eldest of a family of five, was asked what he thought was the best means of relieving family tensions. He replied: 'Everybody knowing what to expect in a family program so that no one's plans are unexpectedly upset by any or all the rest of the family.'" [4] This is good hard sense and should be adhered to as far as possible in every home.

Parents also need to spend proper time with their children, especially with boys. Fathers tend to neglect this angle of parent-child relations. Boys often feel the need of their fathers keenly as Myers has observed: "Many a boy in his teens feels as if he were an orphan wishing that he had a father like the father of his pal. He wants a dad who understands him, who will not laugh at him when he tells about his troubles, who will make him feel he cares to hear anything he wants to tell him." [5]

Not only must a father be with his sons, but he must also look to what *kind* of father he will be. It is important that he be the kind of man whom the son is not ashamed to introduce or see on demonstration. And when the boy needs advice and counsel, he needs a dad who will give it. Myers has commented:

> When he has doubts about his physical condition or sex development or has sex worries, he will come to his father as his sympathetic, comforting confessor. No advertisement will lure him to the office of a quack. From his dad he will learn how to take care of himself and how to live a clean and manly life with healthy attitudes toward girls. His dad will guide him in good physical and mental health, encourage him to cultivate wide friendships with other boys and girls, to engage

[3] H. H. Remmers and D. H. Radlers, *The American Teenager*, n.p.
[4] G. C. Myers, *Marriage and Parenthood*, pp. 232, 233.
[5] *Ibid.*, p. 259.

in outdoor sports and athletics and to acquire wide interests outside himself. [6]

This same good sense can be applied to the mother-daughter relationship by simply substituting mother-daughter for dad and son in the above passage.

Some parents carry this idea of being with their children too far and try to become their teen-agers' "pals." Mothers especially do this at times with mother-daughter dresses and outfits. However, young people do not need us as pals but as *parents;* normal youngsters have their pals among their peers. What they need at home is understanding, sympathetic and sometimes stern parents who can not only tell them what and how about life, but *show* them how to live it successfully in daily demonstration.

Chapter 8

Mastering Money

Money is as old as the higher civilizations. In most ancient times, food, clothing, cattle, horses and other such things were used as a medium of exchange. With the development of higher civilizations in which men moved about or traveled to trade and make their way in life, some forms of exchange of values other than the above became a necessity. Later, coins of the more precious metals — gold, silver and so on — were made for use in exchange, and have continued till now.

The Bible has much to say about money. Someone has said money is mentioned equivalent to almost every third verse in the Bible. Proverbs is a rich book for youth in instruction about the use of money. Every young person should read Proverbs with money in mind and get lessons regarding it.

In many ways money both governs a man's life and reveals just what kind of person he is by his use of it. The Apostle Paul warned

[6] *Ibid.,* p. 260.

that "The *love* of money is the root of all evil . . . " (I Tim. 6:10). Someone has said, "Money will buy everything in the world but happiness, and is a passport to everywhere in the universe but heaven." This truth has been well demonstrated both in the Bible and by the history of civilizations.

How children are taught to handle money will govern their success or failure quite largely in life, and is almost equally true of girls as well as boys. If a girl has no proper sense of the value of money, she may wreck her husband and destroy her home later in life. An old time proverb says, "A woman can throw more out the window than a man can bring in at the door." It is also true that "a wasteful woman can break the wealthiest man." To a large extent the success or failure of every man is the measure of his wife's ability to understand and appreciate money values. Boys who have never understood monetary values cannot hope to succeed in life unless they learn the hard way.

There are three major areas which every person should properly understand about money: how to *make* money; how to *save* money; how to *use* money. It is reported that a man took his friend to hear John Wesley preach on a certain occasion. The sermon was on "The Christian and Money." Wesley observed that one should make all the money he could, and that he should save all he could. The man complimented the sermon highly up to this point. But when Wesley gave his third proposition — everyone should *give* all he could — the man exclaimed, "Now he has ruined a good sermon!" There are too many people like this man.

If anyone of the above three propositions is out of balance in one's relationship to money, he is not properly adjusted to life. Parents, then, should try to inculcate these three simple principles into their children's lives and ways of thinking about money. They may do so in several ways, but individual discovery of the best ways to use and benefit from these principles is needful for the best implementation in individual family situations.

1. *Make all the money you can.* Contrary to public opinion, the Bible nowhere condemns anyone for being wealthy. The mere act of being rich is in itself no evil. In fact, the Old Testament promises temporal blessings to those who serve God acceptably out of a godly heart. It is reported that Abraham was a wealthy man (Gen. 13:2). Job, one of the best of the saints in the Old Testament, was termed "the greatest of all the men of the east" (Job 1:3). The statement follows his assessment of possessions and doubtless means the "richest" of all the eastern men. Joseph of Arimathea is said to have been both a disciple of Jesus and a "rich man" (Matt. 27:57).

It is understood that he owned tin mines in what is now Southern England, and that the first Christian church to be built above ground was erected there in the first century. It is true that not many rich and mighty are among the most spiritual Christians, but this does not mean they could not be. Besides, some of God's saints who have done much for His cause have been among the wealthy.

When William Colgate was a poor lad selling soap on the street, it is reported that an old Christian one day said to him something like this: "Son, if you will make a good pound of soap, sell it for a right price, and give God the tenth, He will prosper you." Colgate took that bit of advice literally. As he grew to manhood his soap business also grew. He added toothpaste to his line and made millions of dollars, but he still followed the advice to give God the tenth. In his later years he gave God far more than the tenth. It is reported that R. G. LeTourneau gave to God's cause nearly ninety percent of his income. He has made millions of dollars.

Making money is an art which almost anyone can learn if he is willing to put his head to it. One does not have to be wealthy to become a success. Most wealthy people, when young, were poor. Making money — except by one's brawn and brain — and the use of money, are tied almost inseparably together.

2. *Save all you can.* Possibly the art of making money is more largely revealed in the ability one has to save and use it than in merely making it. Economy is as ancient as mankind. Jesus taught this principle in the miracle of the loaves and fishes. He asked that the "fragments" be gathered up. It is this principle of conservation — saving what is left over from any operation — that counts.

Children need to be taught *economy* and frugality. There is no grace or charity revealed in wastefulness. God is ever so liberal in giving us all things freely to enjoy, but He is also economical in that He wastes nothing. Even the falling leaves of the trees go back to enrich the soil, as does the flower that fades and the weeds and grass that perish. Wastefulness is condemned and economy rewarded by all of nature; and so the lessons in the Bible are meant to instruct us in the same thing.

Children should be taught that out of all they receive, a certain portion is to be saved. First, they should honor the Lord with their substance by setting aside a tithe for His cause and an offering of love. No matter how small the money earned, this system needs to be lovingly inculcated into their minds. Then, they should find some way to save something — even if it be only a few pennies, it helps to inculcate this principle into the very warp and woof of their lives.

Young people need to learn to "use it up, wear it out, or give it to another," and not to waste anything. Wastefulness is a form of destruction, and destructiveness is not a trait of the best people. Often one sees a wealthy person saving something which seems useless. This is how he became wealthy — by learning that everything of any use has value and should not be wasted.

Sometimes a man is placed in charge of an industrial, educational, or other type of institution. Soon the institution begins to gain and prosper, or it begins to lose money and becomes economically unsound. Generally, if the personal life of the individual in charge is investigated closely, it will reveal the secret of the success or failure of the institution. The manner in which a person handles his own affairs is reflected in his work.

Young people who work should endeavor to *save something* out of every pay check, as a rule. This principle of economy will pay dividends when they are married and on their own. The art of saving is as Christian as that of proper giving. No one can ever hope to be successful in life who does not master the art of saving as he grows into maturity. Those who are wasteful as young people will likely go through life in want.

Carelessness about finances can breed all sorts of family ills and difficulties. Money stands high on the list of causes for divorce. Fusses over finances in the home can soon cool the loving ardor that seemed so bright at the marriage altar. I once counseled a couple for several years, helping to hold them together. They were perfectly adjusted as lovers and had a most ideal life. Their children were not problems (this too is high on the list of causes for divorce). But, alas, they could not solve their *money problem*. It finally drove them apart and into a divorce. This example can be duplicated thousands of times over, everywhere.

There are helpful books on how to save money. Go to the library, secure several of these, and start to use the methods outlined, if you wish to save money. Here are a few money-saving hints for parents which, incidentally, need to be taught to the children as well.

(a) *Learn how to save legitimately on income tax deductions.* Each year millions of dollars are lost which could have been saved had the persons been more careful to claim their legitimate deductions. Get a tax saving guide from Christian Economics Foundation, 250 West 57th Street, New York, N.Y., 10019. It will be most helpful in this area.

(b) *Avoid installment buying where possible.* Sometimes there are hidden carrying charges and taxes that may run as high as twelve to fifteen percent or even more. Many times one can pay as much as twelve percent interest in carrying charges on a car. The same is true with major household appliances. Secure a loan at a bank, which will give you the lowest possible interest rate, if you must borrow.

The very best method is to do without many of these conveniences until you can *pay cash* for them. The author knows a minister who is not in the high income bracket but who has paid cash for every new car and all major household appliances for many years. He places in savings and collects interest until he has the cash to buy later. For example, after he purchased his first old used car for cash, he made payments on his next car *in advance,* in savings where the money collected interest until the next car was needed. He has used this method across the years, and in this way, he is *making money* on every car and appliance he owns! Anyone can do this with just a little *self-will* and ingenuity. Do you not see what will happen when this man is old? He will have the accumulated interest of a lifetime, which would have been literally *wasted* to no purpose had he followed the installment buying plan followed by millions.

(c) *Do not live above your income.* Some people are in debt all the time and can never quite make ends meet. They furnish their homes with extravagant furniture, drive cars they cannot afford, wear clothes above their income bracket, eat the most expensive food, and will die long before their time, worrying over their predicament!

Most likely these people have a high sense of insecurity. They want people to think well of them, and they desire to impress people. A quarter's worth of common sense applied to their lives would teach them that most of their better friends are pitying them instead of admiring them, and that they could have the approbation they so much desire much less expensively and lastingly, if they would only live more sensibly. If they learned a few lessons of economy and how to save, they could have the things they want and yet be happy and live free from strain.

(d) *Learn to live well within your income and save a little.* If people would only use their heads to *think,* how much wiser and better they would be. Someone has said that five percent of the people do the thinking for the other ninety-five percent; and that's why the five percent are rich, and the ninety-five percent in such a predicament! God gave you a head to think with — *use it!*

Here is a helpful little gimmick for saving money: In purchasing clothes, groceries, and many other commodities, one pays much more for the "name brands." The same pineapple, which is just as good as the famous name brand, can be had for several cents less per can, for instance. Often less prestigious foods, clothes, household goods and other items are equally as good as those sold under famous name brands for which you pay extra. Incidentally, *you pay* for the advertising of these "name brands," not their companies! Is the prestige worth the price?

Finally, just *use your head* and you can save money at almost every turn you make. In time, you can become much better off as a family.

3. *Give all you can.* Children should be taught the blessing of giving. Paul quoted Jesus in a statement not in the Gospels, "It is more blessed to give than to receive" (Acts 20:35). *Giving* is the heart of the Christian faith. Jesus came not to be ministered to, but to minister, He said, and to "give his life a ransom for many" (Mark 10:45).

Children should be taught to tithe to the Lord their income, not as an essential part of their religion, necessarily, but as an honored privilege. Tithing is the most sensible and reasonable financial system for supporting God's cause. It imposes no heavier burden on the wealthy than upon the poor; it is equally distributed to all income brackets and has attached to it the promises of the Lord (Mal. 3:9, 10). Apparently our Lord never revoked the blessed privilege of tithing, although He did not include it as a necessity for salvation. Whatever one's belief about tithing, it has been held by the church in general as a good means of supporting God's work throughout the Christian centuries. One will never hear a conscientious tither complain about the burden of this method, but many have witnessed to its blessedness in their lives.

(a) *Children should learn that stewardship is a part of the Christian heritage.* Not only is the tithe the Lord's, but all we possess is the Lord's. Sometimes there are Christians who claim to believe in stewardship as their Christian view of money, but they reject tithing as a method of support for God's cause. Many times such people are so tight-fisted with God that He has difficulty getting anything of any consequence out of them for His cause! This type of individual is in a poor position to teach a child anything about the liberality of vital Christianity.

Our time, talents, abilities and our all belong to God. We should teach our children that they must stand ready to give to God whatever He may demand of them, whether in one or another of these areas of life.

(b) *Young people who have been taught the simple lesson to give to God's cause are generally much more tender hearted and compassionate in life than those who were never so taught.* To allow a child to grow up in the home never giving anything is to allow him to be greedy, selfish and often hard-hearted where others are concerned. It is to his own good as a developing personality to learn that giving is an art all men should cherish and practice.

(c) *Giving brings to the giver a sense of value and personal worth.* These feelings are highly desirable in personality development. Personal worth feelings as contrasted with feelings of guilt and self-criticism are much better for the developing young person. Through giving, this great lesson of life — that all men need to share with each other — is taught in the best possible way.

Let us not forget that *one measure of a person's life is the measure of how he handles and uses his money.* This truism is one that will be proven correct in dealing with people the world over.

These wise words from Henry A. Bowman about managing money matters in the home seem a fitting conclusion for this chapter:

> There are several possible methods of handling the actual spending. This is related to, but not identical with, the formulation of the budget. Not all ways are of equal merit. Each couple must decide . . . which way is best adapted to their desires, abilities and temperaments.
>
> (1) One person may handle all money. (2) One may handle all and give the other a personal allowance. (3) The husband may handle some items, the wife others. (4) The husband may handle some items, the wife others, and in addition each may have a personal allowance. (5) One may handle regular expenses, such as rent and utilities, both drawing upon a joint bank account for personal expense. (6) They may at the beginning of each week or month, depending upon how their income is received, apportion their money for various items, paying some immediately and putting into special envelopes the sums reserved for others. . . . (7) In place of envelopes, which necessitates having money about the house, checks may be written in advance, to be cashed when necessary. If the couple have an inclination toward simple bookkeeping, a lump sum may be left in the bank but appropriate to various accounts in a small ledger, then as money is spent for any particular item, it is deducted from the balance in that special account in the family books. (8) Other schemes will suggest [themselves] to the reader who has the determination to keep finances under control and the ingenuity to make control not only effective but interesting. [1]

---

[1] Henry A. Bowman, *Marriage for Moderns*, pp. 399, 400.

Chapter 9

Matters About Marriage

At the rate our American homes are breaking up in divorces, it behooves parents to do everything they can to lay a solid foundation for lasting marriages in their children's future homes. Possibly the most that can be done for future marriages can be done by parents in the home. Doubtless, the broken homes of children may be a contributing factor to other wrecked homes when those children become adults. "Like father, like son" may be a pattern followed sometimes, although in many cases children from broken homes are more determined than the average to make a success of marriage. However this may be, it is certain that the home is the ideal place to lay the cultural foundations for success in marriage.

Parents truly interested in helping prepare their young people for marriage will find the following points extremely helpful:

1. *Try to make a happy home for the children.* Happy homes generate the desire in children to duplicate them in their own homes. Make much of every birthday, holiday and special occasion. Help the children to learn to accept responsibility; to live normally; to try to develop good habits of work, etiquette, health, education, and to get along well with each other.

Buy many good books and give the children music lessons if possible. Teach them the value of money and its use; give them exposure to as many fine people as possible by having such persons visit in your home. Take them to centers of learning and to religious activities such as summer camps, conventions, Christian song festivals and other such places. Purchase religious cultural records for them; take them to museums of art and other cultural places. Give them the broadest and best advantages in all legitimate things you can afford, and help them to enjoy home life. Develop in them deep loyalty to the home, the church, the state and nation. National patriotism is right and good. Love for their land and respect for their leaders and their flag are important facets of children's lives.

Make the home as nearly as possible not only a shelter from the storms of life, but also a library, a training center, a university and a hallowed sanctuary of worship to God. Maintain the family altar and give the children a solid Christian education in home Bible study as much as possible.

2. *Give children good training about courtship and marriage.* If you feel unqualified for this task, find good books along these lines and encourage the young people to read them. There is no better friend to youth than a good book about such matters. Ignorance of proper conduct during dating times and courtship and preparation for marriage can often lead to lifelong sorrow. These matters are too important for any young person to be ignorant about them.

3. *Give young people all the aid you can during dating times.* Homes in the past had what was called a "parlor," separated from the rest of the home by being more or less isolated. It was a place which was not passed through by everyone on his way to some other part of the house. Here girls entertained their boyfriends in privacy. This was one of the finest rooms American homes ever had. It was a sad day for youth when it became unfashionable. Now girls have no suitable place, generally, to be with their dates in the home, so long trips from home in a car, often ending in parking in seclusion, have resulted. Here the girl is often at the mercy of the boy. If he is a gentleman she is reasonably safe; if not, the worst can happen. While double dating by two or more couples may be protective, often it is not. Many times young people choose another pair whom they know are all of one mind about extremes in petting and sex play, then all feel safe, no matter what happens.

When possible, parents should provide space in the living room or family room in which a girl may entertain her dates. Since, however, current dating is primarily centered around activities outside the home, the mother must instruct her daughter in the proper methods of conduct — what is allowable and what is not — on dates. Sons also should be instructed early in the correct rules of conduct with girls they date. If these rules are instilled into the young properly, they will go far toward helping them to avoid unbecoming behavior. Such rules are quite simple. It should be understood by all youth that such things as holding hands, placing the arm lightly around the shoulder of the girl friend, and other becoming ways of showing affection are all right. A greeting and parting kiss that is light may be allowed, if not overindulged until it arouses passion. This is not good for any couple. But matters of handling and fondling other parts of the body and any form of sex play are strictly taboo and should *never* be permitted by the girl nor attempted by the boy. Not even engaged couples should allow such intimacies. They are unethical and un-Christian and they are dangerous. Besides, they cannot possibly bring any good. Often they result in deep guilt complexes which hinder and inhibit the wife, especially, in love-making after marriage. Premarital intimacies are often the reason for a wife's frigidity after marriage. Ministers and counselors meet the results of such misconduct again and again in marriage problems which result from it.

4. *Young people, choose your friends wisely.* It is hoped that young people will read this section carefully. Always see that as a Christian you date only Christians. If you are not a Christian, remember it is a serious thing to even think of marriage outside of Christ. You may make a lifetime mistake for which you will pay dearly. Come to Him and ask for His guidance in this matter above all. Dr. Orr has said: "Christian girls should marry only in the bonds of their faith. In other words, Protestants should marry Protestants, and Catholics the same. Both ministers and priests are agreed on this. The systems are far too diverse to allow compatibility. Much misery can be averted if this rule is followed." [1] The same applies to boys of course. Also, one should marry within even a closer sense of his own religious communion. Those with differences as Calvinists and Arminians (for example, those of a Baptist and a Methodist background) will often find some difficulty arising out of their differences of beliefs. Generally, people are happier if they marry within their own denominational faith — or at least within the general framework of their belief.

So long as the boy or girl meets religious and other important requirements, do not be too choosy about minor matters. This advice is illustrated from one of Ann Landers' columns in the *Los Angeles Herald-Examiner*:

> *Dear Ann:* When I started to date I wouldn't consider going with anyone who wasn't at least five feet ten, well-built and handsome. I made fun of the boys who were a little too fat or a little too thin. If a fellow's nose was too big or his teeth weren't straight, he was automatically off my list.
>
> A boy's clothes were important, too. If he didn't look like a fashion model I wouldn't consider being seen with him. My mother warned me I was making a big mistake, but I wouldn't listen. I made fun of her, too. Guess what happened! I married the best looking, best-

[1] William W. Orr, *How to Get a Husband,* p. 4.

dressed fellow in town. All the girls were green with envy. Our wedding pictures were great.

We now have five children. My handsome, well-dressed husband never takes me anywhere, not even to church. I haven't eaten in a restaurant for three years. He prefers to go places alone.

I am disgusted and fed up, but I am determined to keep our marriage together. This rotten husband happens to be a good father.

Please warn the girls out there in Dateland not to pass up the short, homely fellows. I'm sorry I didn't have sense enough to grab one for myself.
— Susan

Dear Susan: You're so right. Marrying for looks is a lot like buying wax fruit. You can starve to death looking at it.

Dr. Orr makes another good suggestion to youth about selecting a mate:

Talk the matter over frankly and completely with good old Dad and Mother. If there is any spot where you need honest, unprejudiced, unselfish down-to-earth advice, it's at this point. Now don't get any silly notions about your parents being prejudiced. They want the best for you. They want you to get married, but they want your marriage to be a success. [2]

Many a heartache could have been avoided if young people had taken this bit of good advice. Your parents know far more about such things than you now feel they know. Their advice will often prove invaluable.

In one of Dr. Billy Graham's columns in the *Los Angeles Herald-Examiner,* there appeared some sound advice to courting couples tempted to go too far with intimacies:

Q — According to the Bible are sexual intimacies, aside from intercourse, wrong, if they are deep and intimate expressions of true love before marriage?
— M.S.

A young person in love is confronted with a real problem. His physical being cries out for expression and every nerve and fiber demands intimacy with his beloved. But, as I have said over and over, expressions of love prior to holy matrimony require discipline and restraint.

If proper respect for your beloved is not maintained, the whole structure of love breaks down and it dissipates into the common thing called lust. Many marriages are ruined before the marriage ceremony is performed because the restraint which is a part of true love is not exercised.

This is why the Bible urges young people to "flee from youthful

[2] William W. Orr, *How to Get Along With Your Parents,* p. 16.

lusts." Through this admonition the Lord is trying to perpetuate the warm glow of real love and guard against it becoming a thing on the mere animal plane. Wise and happy are the young people who heed it.

The Scriptures are clear at this point: "Love doth not behave itself unseemly, seeketh not her own, thinketh no evil. . . . rejoiceth not in iniquity, but rejoiceth in the truth; beareth all things, hopeth all things, endureth all things."

These were written for your happiness. Believe me!

Those who heed these words of counsel will live to prove they are right. They will also avoid bitter sorrows which those who do not take the advice will surely meet.

Young people between the ages of fifteen and twenty should read many books on courtships and marriage and preparation for marriage. If there are courses open to them on these subjects, especially in Christian schools, they should by all means take these. Even in the secular schools such courses may be beneficial.

Dr. Clyde M. Narramore's book, *Happiness in Marriage,* is recommended. It may be secured at the Narramore Christian Foundation, 1409 N. Walnut Grove Avenue, Rosemead, California. *Problems of Modern Youth,* by the author and wife, available from Deal Publications, 11326 Ranchito St., El Monte, California, is also recommended.

English and Pearson have given some good advice to those seeking a mate. They warn: "Few young people seem to know what to look for in choosing a mate. The one they want often does not turn out to be the one they need."[3] This is why youth needs counsel in such an important matter.

Here are the results of a survey by the well-known marriage counselor, Clifford Adams, as to the most desirable traits of persons chosen as mates, listed by a group of college students:

Put first by single men:		*Put first by single young women:* [4]	
Companionship	40%	Love	33%
Sexual satisfaction	30%	Security	27%
Love	15%	Companionship	20%
Children	10%	Children	11%
Home	5%	Sexual satisfaction	9%

The men do not even mention "security," and there is a large gap between matters of love, companionship and sexual satisfaction. This survey shows that men and women are looking for different things as priorities in marriage. For instance, 30 percent of the men

[3] O. S. English and G. J. Pearson, *Emotional Problems of Living,* p. 429.
[4] *Ibid.,* p. 430.

thought sexual satisfaction was very important, whereas only 9 percent of the women would put it first.

Dr. Adams suggests that the couple consider the following ten points in the matter of mate-selection.

> Will this mate: Bring you social approval? Offer security? Help you get ahead? Embarrass you by nonconformity? Be affectionate to you? Be interested in your work? Share your feeling about children? Satisfy you sexually? Work hard to make your marriage a success? Talk things over with you?

Adams suggests that if he comes short in these matters, one had better do more courting and looking around! Life is too serious to ruin it by getting the wrong mate. He warns that: "Courtship is a process of exploring a man and a woman's personality rather than an attempt to win each other by each party concealing his less attractive traits. Courtship should be an honest search for the suitable mate." [5]

Another good way in which to test personality likenesses and differences and to discover whether or not a couple will get along in marriage is what I have called the Twenty-twenty Test. List ten things you *like* or enjoy doing and then ten things you do not like. Have your boy or girl friend make a similar list. These lists should cover all major phases of life such as religion, recreation, food, education, money, sex, children, home and so on. Keep a copy of your two lists and give a copy to your friend, in exchange for his two copies. Now, grade these copies against each other. If you come out finding out there are as many as ten things which you like that he does not like, or you do not like, which he likes, *you had better do a lot more courting!* It is likely you will have an unhappy marriage. This simple test is an eye-opener. The test should be made in "judgment day honesty" if it is to really mean anything.

5. *Youthful marriages should be avoided.* Parents should start from early years to educate their children to finish college if possible, or at least secure the needed training in some field to provide well for the mate before marriage. Girls especially should be well prepared to make a good living without a husband. A girl can have no better insurance than a teacher's certificate, a nursing degree, or at least training from a good business college. If her husband dies or becomes crippled for life, she can then make a good living for the family. Without such training she is at the mercy of relatives or state aid, which at best is poor provision for rearing a family.

[5] *Ibid.*, p. 431.

Dr. Orr has some excellent counsel on the matter of early marriage:

> There will be occasions when young people who have known each other all their lives, and whose parents agree, will want to become serious, perhaps when they are 18 or 19. But speaking generally, I would say that the matter of having a steady boy friend or girl friend should be put off until the twentieth year or after. And do you know I have the weight of sober statistics behind me. Marriages are happier and last longer when the young people do not become engaged until they reach a sensible age. On the other hand, tragedy strikes more often and there are far more heartaches and broken homes in the wake of too early marriages. Read the statistics for yourself. [6]

Parents and young people alike should take this advice seriously, for the future happiness of young people is at stake. Marriages in the middle and late teens are generally unsuccessful as statistics show. Here are several sensible reasons why marriages too early are unwise:

(1) *Youthful parents are far from emotionally mature enough to rear a child.* They may warp its personality for all time to come and may even lay the foundation for its eternal ruin. To start a soul upon its eternal course is far too serious a *matter for two teenagers as parents to assume.* They have not even been finally and completely reared themselves, and yet they start to assume one of the most heavy and serious responsibilities God can give a human being — procreating and rearing another being! Youthful marriages may produce eternally tragic consequences.

(2) *Such marriages rob youth of natural, normal teen-age life.* This in itself is an abnormality. It often produces sad consequences in later life. Who has not seen the teen-age married woman or man, when in their mid-thirties they should be settled down to normal adult life, living and acting like teen-agers? Sometimes such parents embarrass their children no end. I recall now such a woman who raced her husband's car around town, careening around corners, screeching tires and generally acting like a teen-ager. She dressed like a teen-ager and was as fickle as any teen-ager. Her teen-age daughter was often embarrassed by her and sometimes showed more intelligent adult behavior than her mother did! Boys who marry in the teens often show these same characteristics in later life. They are merely trying to recapture the life they lost in their teen years by a too serious, too adult adjustment to life too early.

(3) *Even more serious is the fact that such young people are incapable of making the choices of mates they will want to be living*

[6] William W. Orr, *How to Get a Husband*, p. 16.

with when they are adults. A girl, seventeen or eighteen years of age or a boy of eighteen or nineteen will naturally choose a certain type of person. But the sad part is if such a young person should remain single, they would not be caught dead with the same *type* of person — maybe not with the same individual — at twenty-two and twenty-four years of age! But if they are married to them, there is nothing to do but try to readjust to an adult situation and make the best of it. They will likely never be as happy as they might have been had they waited awhile to choose a mate.

Of course there is always the avenue of divorce as a means of getting out of an undesirable situation. But divorce has never been and never will be the answer. Sadly, there *is* no proper answer to the follies of a youthful, unfortunate marriage. Divorce only leaves deep emotional scars, bitter memories, a sense of futility and failure. It but paves the way for another and often even *more unstable* marriage. Marriage is for keeps — divorce is not the answer. (See the author's tract, *Don't Get a Divorce.*) Even the young widowed person is never the same again. There is no road back to the state of singleness, no matter what one may do.

Even in the case of pre-marital pregnancies, it is most advisable to give the child away for adoption and remain single. Statistics support this position. If such a teen-age couple may later decide to marry when each is older and they are adult enough to know what they *want* in a marriage, fine. This may be a wonderful thing. But never marry as a hasty way to legalize an already sinful and indulgent act! It seldom ever works out right. Most likely it will end in divorce, and the latter evil will be as bad or even worse than the former. In earlier days, forced marriage often worked, but it will not work well in our times. The mores and folkways of earlier times tended to hold such marriages together, but our modern mores make divorce far too easy, and too often the couple takes what appears like the easiest way out. Generally, it is not good advice to youth to marry to cover up such a mistake.

(4) *The high divorce rates resulting from teen marriages also argue against them.* Several factors may here be considered, not the least of which is the following: People in the *lower income* bracket show the *highest* rate of divorce! Teen-agers are always in the lower income bracket. Marriage too often seals the doom of a couple for much further training, by which means alone, generally, the income can be increased. A survey showed that three times as many teen-age wives and four times as many teen-age husbands get divorces as those who wait until later to marry. (See *McCalls* Magazine, August, 1966, article on teen-age marriages.)

Statistics from *The Student Outlook*, published by the *Los Angeles Times*, for the Fall of 1966 show that "50 percent of all marriages involving a teen-ager end in divorce within five years." These statistics remain as true in 1970 as they were then. These are sad but frightfully sobering facts which young people need to face. Unfortunately, most young people who decide to marry too young feel they can "beat the statistics." They just don't do it. There are certain laws of averages which cannot be defied. It is folly to try to beat the game, and ruin your life in the attempt.

Of the fifty percent that manage to stay married longer than five years, many divorce after that time. Many more who do stay together live lives of fussing, quarreling and disagreeing in general. Some feel religiously and morally bound to each other — which is right — but their homes are a *hell on earth!*

Again, often the young bride becomes a mother far too early. Her health is broken by having too many children at too young an age. When she is in her mid-thirties and ought to be strong and healthy, her health is wrecked. She is not a suitable sexual partner for her husband, who is in his prime and *needs* a suitable sex partner. The result is all sorts of frustrations for them both. If the husband is not a Christian, the temptation to "step out" on his wife is often great, and many times he does just that. The whole picture is one of sadness and pity. Often children of such early marriages grow up maladjusted, emotionally sick, and are problems for themselves and for society. Can two young people seriously consider the tragedy of giving the world such children? Often such children become criminals or maladjusted wives or husbands, spreading more misery into other lives.

The whole business of premature marriages is fraught with such tragic consequences that it seems any sane, thinking young person would never want to enter into such a marriage.

Often the major motive for the boy in such a marriage is sexual satisfaction. Unfortunately, he is often disappointed in this area, for the girl is neither sexually nor emotionally mature enough to offer a completely happy, satisfying sex life. Normally, girls do not blossom out into their best as sex partners until the middle or late twenties. Boys reach their sexual prime between the ages of eighteen and twenty-five, whereas girls reach their prime generally much later. Some women never reach their best years sexually until their thirties. If you are considering a youthful marriage, you ought to think these things over seriously!

(5) *Compatibility is important in marriage.* One can tie a cat and a dog together by their tails, hang them over a clothesline, and get

a lot of *unity,* but no *harmony!* If marriages are to succeed, there must be a certain amount of harmony. Young people must be taught that ideal marriages are not necessarily those in which there is never a ruffle, but those in which partners settle their differences without destroying either their love or respect for each other.

To find the most compatibility in a marriage, the two partners should come from similar religious and cultural backgrounds. A lifetime farmer and a city slicker, a college graduate and a high school dropout, for instance, may often find difficulty making a good marital adjustment. Such marriages can survive, but with much more difficulty, for they will never fully understand and appreciate each other's viewpoints of life. There are many other such situations not conducive to successful marriages. It is open to serious question whether Negroes and Whites should marry, especially for the sake of the children, who may find great difficulty in meeting their life situations.

When planning marriage, one needs much sober thinking, hard-headed good judgment and a long view of all the consequences.

(6) *Pre-marital counseling is important before any marriage, however well educated and sophisticated the couple may be.* Many books on marriage and sex and children should be read, but even these are often not enough. Several sessions with a good marriage counselor can help a couple to avoid many of the pitfalls which have all but ruined many a marriage before it got started! If the minister is well trained and able to do marriage counseling, he would be the ideal person to go to for pre-marital counseling. If not, then go to a professional marriage and family counselor. Your marriage will get off to a much better start. The first session with the counselor should generally be at least six weeks to two months in advance of marriage, if possible. But if not, even one session only shortly before the marriage is better than none. It is best if the fellow and girl go together. The counselor will generally want to see them together, then each one separately, with possibly a final session together. There are many things which need to be discussed and met face-to-face in such sessions. If the man will *not* go, then the girl should go alone for her own sake. She can often express much of what she receives to her husband. If he objects to any pre-marital counseling either for himself or her, then the girl should seriously consider that she may have a genuine problem on her hands! She may be headed for all kinds of trouble in a marriage with a man who is so obstinate and ignorant as this. It may be well to cool the matter by a postponement of the marriage until they can come to some kind of sensible terms.

Unfortunately, there are still a few young men with the idea that a woman is his "chattel" and he can use her as he wishes, once they are married. For instance, if he wants intercourse five times a week and she feels unable to comply, she may either bow to his wishes or have to tolerate a sullen, sour and uncooperative husband. If he is this type of person, the girl should know this before marriage, if possible. His domineering ways may become evident especially after engagement and near the marriage. Marriage is a cooperative venture in which the wife should have equal say with the husband about most matters. Otherwise there can be little true happiness in the marriage for either of the pair.

(7) *By all means encourage the couple to have a church wedding, or if not, at least a home wedding.* Church weddings add sanctity and dignity to the ceremony and often have a salutary effect upon the young couple. A lovely home wedding will also lend itself to a certain dignity and home atmosphere which is wholesome for the couple. Many sacred memories hover about a wedding for long years to come, when it is done properly.

(8) *If possible the couple should have a home or apartment furnished and ready before marriage.* In this way they can get off to the proper start in their own home. Living with relatives after marriage is almost a sure way to invite troubles for the marriage.

Young people will do much better if they postpone their marriage until they are able to have their own place to live, even though it is only a small rented apartment. Some marriages have weathered the storm of early living with relatives, but many times unpleasantness develops.

By all means the couple should plan to have an income sufficient to provide for all their needs, plus an emergency fund. Pregnancies sometimes occur before they were planned. The couple should be in position to accept this fact without emotional disturbances, quarreling and blaming each other. If there has been adequate fore-planning and proper arrangements, there need to be no difficulties in such an emergency.

(9) *In-laws, stay out of the affairs of your married children.* Give advice and counsel only when you are *asked for it,* not on every occasion when you feel it is necessary. Unsought advice is often *needed,* but seldom *heeded!* Young people have to learn some things the hard way, despite all our loving concern for them.

Accept your in-law son or daughter as your own, but keep them at a respectful distance. Whenever you can properly do so, take sides with the in-law against the son or daughter. In this way, they will come to feel that you are truly impartial and will accept you much better. Don't try to rear the grandchildren or steal their affections. Leave them with their parents, except in cases where for religious or moral guidance you need to help them. Treat your in-laws as you wanted yours to treat you when you were first married, and likely all will turn out well.

Try to be the best, most unselfish grandparents in the world!

PRAYER OF A HOMEMAKER

I thank You, Father, for a home to keep.
Where I, in simple unadorned attire
May satisfy the heart's age-old desire
To daily bake and cleanse and dust and sweep.
I thank You, Father, for the love I reap
In fields of duty where I often tire,
But where, relaxed before contentment's fire,
I yield at night to gentle arms of sleep.
I thank You, Father, for Your presence here
In this, my home — my citadel on earth.
With You beside me I need never fear
The many trials to which day gives birth
Or constant tribulations that appear
Upon life's scene to shadow joy and mirth.

— Lydia O. Jackson, in *Guideposts*

BIBLIOGRAPHY AND SUGGESTED READING LIST

Benson, Clarence H. *An Introduction to Child Study*. Chicago: Moody Press, 1942.

Blood, R. O., and D. M. Wolfe. *Husbands and Wives, the Dynamic of Married Living*. Glencoe, Illinois: The Free Press, 1960.

Bowman, Henry A. *Marriage for Moderns*. New York: McGraw-Hill Book Company, Inc., 1954.

Brandt, Henry, and H. E. Dowdy. *Building a Christian Home*. Wheaton, Illinois: Scripture Press, 1960.

Brandt, Henry. *Keys to Better Living for Parents*. Chicago: Moody Press, 1958.

Deal, William S. *A Happy Married Life and How to Live It*. Grand Rapids, Michigan: Zondervan Publishing House, 1963.

Deen, Edith. *Family Living in the Bible*. New York: Harper and Row, 1963.

De Jong, Alexander C. *The Christian Family and Home*. Grand Rapids, Michigan: Baker Book House, 1959.

Duvall, Evelyn Millis. *Building Your Marriage*. New York: Public Affairs Pamphlets, 1964.

English, O. S., and G. J. Pearson. *Emotional Problems of Living*. New York: W. W. Norton and Company, third edition, 1963.

Ernst, Morris L., and David Loth. *For Better or Worse*. New York: Harper, 1951 and 1952.

Evans, Louis H. *Your Marriage — Duel or Duet*. Westwood, New Jersey: Fleming H. Revell, n.d.

Family Circle. April, June, 1967.

Friend, Nellie E. *Love and You*. New York: Fleming H. Revell, n.d.

Geiseman, O. A. *Make Yours a Happy Marriage*. St. Louis: Concordia Publishing House, 1946.

Hall, Winfield Scott. *Love and Marriage*. Philadelphia: John C. Winston Co., 1929.

Howell, Roy W. *The Christian Home*. Winona Lake, Ind.: Light and Life Press, 1965.

Hendricks, William C. *God's Temples*. Grand Rapids, Michigan: William B. Eerdmans, 1966.

Hubbard, L. R. *Dianetics, The Modern Science of Mental Health*. New York: Hermitage, 1950.

Jacobs, Vernon J. *Starlight Talks to Youth*. Grand Rapids, Michigan: Baker Book House, 1961.

Landis, Judson R., and Mary Landis. *Marriage and Family Living*. Englewood Cliffs, N.J.: Prentice Hall, 1960.

————. *Building a Successful Marriage*. Englewood Cliffs, N.J.: Prentice Hall, 1958.

Lewin, S.A., and John Gilmore. *Sex Without Fear*. New York: Medical Research Press, 1951.

Miles, H.J. *Sexual Happiness in Marriage*. Grand Rapids, Michigan: Zondervan Publishing House, 1968.

Miller, B.F., and J.J. Burt. *Good Health, Personal and Community*. Philadelphia: W.B. Saunders Company, second edition, 1966.

Myers, G.C. *Marriage and Parenthood*. New York: World Publishing Company, 1934.

Narramore, Clyde M. *Happiness in Marriage*. Grand Rapids, Michigan: Zondervan Publishing House, 1961.

————. *How to Tell Your Children About Sex*. Grand Rapids, Michigan: Zondervan Publishing House, 1958.

O'Briane, John A. *Happy Marriage*. New York: Popular Library Books, n.d.

Orr, William W. *Bible Hints on Rearing Children*. Wheaton, Illinois: Scripture Press, 1955.

————. *Can High School Young People Think?* Wheaton, Illinois: Scripture Press, n.d.

————. *God's Answer to Young People's Problems*. Wheaton, Illinois: Scripture Press, n.d.

————. *How to Get Along With Your Parents*. Wheaton, Illinois: Scripture Press, 1958.

————. *How to Get a Husband*. Wheaton, Illinois: Scripture Press, 1953.

————. *How to Keep Your Husband Happy*. Wheaton, Illinois: Scripture Press, 1958.

————. *How to Keep Your Wife Happy*. Wheaton, Illinois: Scripture Press, 1958.

————. *How to Pick a Wife*. Wheaton, Illinois: Scripture Press, 1953.

————. *How to Tell If You're in Love*. Wheaton, Illinois: Scripture Press, n.d.

————. *Love, Courtship and Marriage*. Wheaton, Illinois: Scripture Press, n.d.

————. *Plain Talk About Love and Sex*. Wheaton, Illinois: Scripture Press, n.d.

————. *Seven Rules for a Happy Christian Home*. Wheaton, Illinois: Scripture Press, n.d.

————. *What the Bible Says About Divorce*. Glendale, California: The Church Press, n.d.

————. *What Every Christian Boy Should Know*. Wheaton, Illinois: Scripture Press, n.d.

————. *What Every Christian Girl Should Know*. Wheaton, Illinois: Scripture Press, n.d.

————. *What Every Christian Husband Should Know*. Wheaton, Illinois: Scripture Press, 1963.

————. *What Every Christian Wife Should Know.* Wheaton, Illinois: Scripture Press, 1963.

————. *What To Teach Young Children.* Wheaton, Illinois: Scripture Press, 1966.

————. *Your Christian Wedding.* Wheaton, Illinois: Scripture Press, 1955.

Peale, Norman Vincent. *Sin, Sex and Self-Control.* Carmel, N. Y.: Guideposts Associated, 1965.

Phillips, Jean C. *Better Homes and Gardens Baby Book.* Des Moines, Iowa: n.d.

Popenoe, Paul. *Marriage Before and After.* New York: Wilfred Funk, Inc., 1943.

————. *Preparing for Marriage.* Los Angeles: American Institute of Family Relations, 1938.

Remmers, H. H. and D. H. Radlers. *The American Teen-ager.* Indianapolis: Bobbs-Merrill, 1957.

Ruch, Floyd L. *Psychology and Life.* Chicago: Scott, Foresman and Company, fifth edition, 1958.

Sentman, E. A. *Child Training, a Guide to Successful Parenthood.* Lake Bluff, Illinois: Child Development, Inc., n.d.

Shaw, Doreen, and Bertha Johnson. *Your Children.* Chicago: Moody Press, 1957.

Simon, Martin P. *Points for Parents.* Grand Rapids: Zondervan Publishing House, 1963.

Stearns, A. E. *The Challenge of Youth.* Boston: W. A. Wild Company, 1963.

The Sunday School Messenger. Indianapolis. June 4, 1967.

Tweedie, Donald F. *Of Sex and Saints.* Grand Rapids, Michigan: Baker Book House, 1965.

Williams, Norman V. *The Christian Home.* Chicago: Moody Press, 1952.

Wyden, Peter and Barbara, *Growing Up Straight, or What Every Parent Should Know About Homosexuality.* New York: Day and Stein, 1968.

Wynn, John Charles. *Sex, Family and Society in Theological Focus.* New York: Association Press, 1966.